POVERTY

YESTERDAY and TODAY

View of a rear tenement in New York in the early 1900's. (photograph by Jacob A. Riis, The Jacob A. Riis Collection, Museum of the City of New York)

POVERTY

YESTERDAY and TODAY

by Sidney Lens

Illustrated with Photographs

Thomas Y. Crowell Company • New York

Copyright © 1973 by Sidney Lens

This book is a revised, updated version of the author's
earlier book *Poverty: America's Enduring Paradox*.

Designed by Celeste Whitney

Manufactured in the United States of America

ISBN 0-690-00182-7

Library of Congress Cataloging in Publication Data

Lens, Sidney.
Poverty: yesterday and today.
  Bibliography: p.
  1. Poor—United States—History.
2. Economic assistance, Domestic—United
States—History. I. Title.
HC110.P6L395   301.44′1   73-5860
ISBN 0-690-00182-7

1 2 3 4 5 6 7 8 9 10

To Sophie,
my mother, the little immigrant
lady who arrived in 1907 and died in 1954
without ever catching the gold ring

Contents

Playground in a tenement alley on New York's Lower East Side. (photograph by Lewis Hine, International Museum of Photography at George Eastman House)

Introduction

The war on poverty is as old as America, but it has not yet been won.

That must seem strange because the United States is rich today beyond the wildest dreams of what was considered possible forty years ago. In 1971 Uncle Sam produced more than a trillion dollars of goods and services—the first nation in history to reach this peak. A trillion is a thousand billion, or a million million; either way it is an enormous sum of money. It means that we produced about $5,000 worth of autos, sewing machines, medical services for every man, woman, and child in the country.

Yet there are still many millions of poor in the United States. And there is no immediate prospect that these millions will soon become un-poor.

That does not mean that the United States has not been the "land of promise." It has. Countless people have come here and made their fortunes. Many more have come here poor and risen to comfortable circumstances. If they didn't succeed, then their children or grandchildren did. The son of a laborer became an affluent lawyer or politician. The son of a small storekeeper became a doctor or professor.

But while poverty ended for some people, there was always a

new group of poor to take their place. And some, such as the blacks, remained poor for hundreds of years, even while America was becoming so rich. Poverty in America has been a cat with nine lives.

One group of Americans escapes from poverty, but the ranks of the poor continue to grow as another group—usually immigrants—replaces them. Poverty shrinks for a while, during good times, then suddenly grows rapidly as a depression spreads unemployment and hunger far and wide.

A thousand books could be written—and have been written—about why this is so. But judge for yourself as the tale of poverty and antipoverty programs unfolds.

1

In Merrie England

Like so much in American life, the story of poverty in this country goes back to England. It was from England that the bulk of immigrant poor came to the Thirteen Colonies. And from England we inherited our ideas on how to deal with poverty. In a certain sense, the settlement of America was Great Britain's "war on poverty."

In the sixteenth and seventeenth centuries the people of England lived, for the most part, in villages. The land they plowed belonged to a landlord, and they paid him rent and did certain types of work for him. Obviously these peasants were poor, but they had a certain amount of security. A peasant who had a bad crop, or who had an accident, could go to his landlord for help. Or he could go to the Church, which was considered a refuge for the hungry.

The peasant also had security in another sense. He didn't own the land he farmed, but he was reasonably sure that he could continue to work it, and that when he died his children would be permitted to work it—after paying a small fee to the landlord. All this was a matter of custom. It was also customary that rents were to remain the same, or only slightly higher, from year to year.

But England just then was in the midst of a boom. For a long time its chief export had been wool, and wool manufacturing in Europe was now expanding rapidly. As the demand for the raw commodity, and the price, kept going up, English landlords found they could make more money raising sheep on their fields than from the rents they charged peasants. So, by devices called "enclosure" and "rack-renting" they took over, for sheep raising, land that for centuries had been farmed by peasants.

By age-old custom each village had a "commons," a piece of land used by everyone, peasant as well as landlord, to graze cattle. The commons was supposed to be commonly owned. But in order to find more pasture land for their sheep, the landlords built enclosures—fences—around this common property and made it their own. Tenants and small farmers now had to graze their cattle elsewhere, or slaughter them. In many cases they were forced to give up their farms.

A 1581 pamphlet complained that "where 40 persons had their livings, now one man and shepherd have all . . . by these enclosures men do lack livings and be idle." As the peasants fled (in many places a quarter to a half of them), the landlord cried "good riddance" and tore down their cottages.

Enclosure continued in England, and to a lesser extent on the European Continent, from the sixteenth to the early nineteenth century. An eighteenth-century ditty, expressing the bitterness of the displaced peasant, went like this:

> The law locks up the man or woman
> Who steals a goose from off the common;
> But leaves the greater villain loose
> Who steals the common from the goose.

Another device for getting rid of peasants was rack-renting. The landlords raised rents and fines sky-high, and tenants who couldn't afford them either gave up their farms or were dispossessed. A 1533 petition by residents of Whitby listed five lords who had increased rents as much as eight times what they used to be.

Peasants left the villages in droves and either starved, or stole or begged to keep body and soul together. Sheffield, whose population in 1615 was 2,207, reported 725 people existing on charity. In Scotland, a member of the parliament stated in 1698 that "the number of beggars . . . is reckoned at not less than 200,000," a high number considering how small populations were at that time.

"The Land growes weary of her Inhabitants," observed a future leader of New England.

A century and a quarter after the enclosures began to make paupers of so many people, England introduced the world's first antipoverty program—Queen Elizabeth's poor laws. Elizabeth, the last of the Tudor monarchs, ruled from 1558 to 1603. In this period England rose to greatness and wealth. It defeated the Spanish Armada and sent adventurers such as Francis Drake throughout the world. This was the age, too, of Shakespeare and Bacon.

But while merchants and landlords were becoming wealthy beyond anything known before, the problem of pauperism was growing apace. There were too many people in want and no place for them to turn—neither to their old landlords nor to the Church.

Previous attitudes to these unfortunate citizens had often been very harsh. An act of 1531 granted men too old to work licenses to beg in fixed places. The same act, however, ordered that able-bodied men who were idle be lashed or imprisoned. A man without work in those days was considered a criminal. He might be tied to a cart tail or whipped, and he was made to take an oath that he would return to his birthplace to find honest labor. For a second offense an ear was cut off, and for the third he might be executed.

An act of 1572 decreed that idlers—"vagrants"—would be put out to one year of service with a property owner, without pay except room and board. If no owner could be found to take him, the "criminal" was to be whipped and have his right ear "burned through to the gristle." For the third offense, death was the punishment.

Giving out tickets for soup to London unemployed. (New York Public Library)

Queen Elizabeth's poor laws of 1601 retained the distinction between the helpless poor—the aged or crippled—and the idle poor. Each parish selected four householders, who with the Church warden acted as "overseers of the poor." For those who were helpless, they granted direct relief in the form of money, food, and shelter. For those who were idle but able-bodied, they bought flax, hemp, wool, and other materials, for the vagrants to spin and weave. Children whose parents could not provide for them were hired out as apprentices.

The poor laws were in many respects a step forward. Whipping of paupers or fining of unlicensed beggars was abolished. Almshouses were set up for the sick and infirm, and children who lived in them were given an education of sorts.

If the attitude toward the able-bodied seems severe, it must be noted, on the other side, that the government felt a strong obligation toward the helpless. In the years 1665–66, when war, plague, and the burning of a large part of London had made one-fifth of England's population paupers, almost half of King Charles II's income from taxes was used for relief.

But liberal as these laws were by the standards of the time, they could not cope with unemployment. Almshouses and forced labor were no substitute for owning a patch of land. For the disadvantaged, therefore, the colonies in America beckoned like a beacon. A ballad sung at the time the first 120 adventurers were leaving for Jamestown in 1606 showed the high hopes of the English poor for the New World. The ballad referred to "Virginia, Earth's only Paradise." A London actor pictured America as a lush land where Indians went "forth on holy days to gather rubies and diamonds by the seashore."

Many thought of America as Sir Thomas More did in his satirical book *Utopia*. The book, written in Latin and published in 1516, relates More's conversations with a mythical sailor, Ralph Hythlodaye, who shipped out to the New World with Amerigo Vespucci. Here he came upon an island of peace and plenty called "Utopia." Everyone had a job, land was owned by all in common, children received public education, and people worked only six hours a day. Hythlodaye contrasted this enchanting place with the appalling poverty of England.

Letting his imagination run on, More envisioned in this great, mysterious, and boundless paradise a final release from the malady wracking England—landlessness. Many millions who later crossed the ocean to a new home, came with the hope they could find their "utopia" there.

For the English monarchy the New World was to be a source of precious metals, furs, timber for the royal navy, and trade. But it was also to be a means of coping with the problem of the jobless.

Sir Humphrey Gilbert, the explorer who first set foot on New-foundland, suggested in 1574 that "we might inhabit some parts of these Countryes [in America] and settle there such needy people of our country which now trouble the commonwealth and through want here at home are enforced to commit out-rageous offences, whereby they are dayly consumed by the gal-lows." One of the stated purposes of the joint stock companies which were given charters to colonize Virginia was to rid Eng-land of its "superfluous twigs." The Spanish minister to England reported to his monarch in 1611 that the "principal reason for colonizing these parts [America] is to give an outlet to so many idle, wretched people as they have in England, and thus prevent the dangers that might be feared of them."

The settlement of America, then, could be considered a war on poverty, though no one in 1611 really thought of it as yet in those words.

2

The Colonial Poor

Sir Francis Drake, after a marauder's trip to South America, landed in a bay north of the present San Francisco in 1572 and named the country he was annexing for Queen Elizabeth, "Nova Albion"—New England. Sir Walter Raleigh more than a decade later arrived with a fleet on the other side of the continent, now North Carolina, and designated it "Virginia"—after the Virgin Queen. By these acts, England claimed most of what is now the United States and Canada.

The English monarchs sliced up America's territorial wealth in large chunks. The area from Maine to the middle of South Carolina, for instance, was granted to two stock companies made up of England's wealthiest businessmen. In return they pledged King James I one-fifth of the gold and silver they expected to find. The charter for the Massachusetts Bay Company was given to twenty-six men, most of them affluent Puritan merchants. The Carolinas went to eight proprietors, including the future Earl of Shaftesbury. Maryland was given to Lord Baltimore and the Calverts; Pennsylvania to William Penn; New York and New Jersey to the Duke of York.

The problem in the New World was to find labor to work these vast territories. There was the Indian of course. But settlers found, to their dismay, that the Indian was too proud to be enslaved. "When they [the Indians] hired themselves out as servants," writes V. F. Calverton, "they did so with the utmost reluctance and upon many occasions robbed and sometimes even killed their masters."

Most of the labor, therefore, was recruited at first from the poor in England. People who were called "crimps" and "newlanders" lured men and women across the ocean by telling them they could find gold and silver in America just for the asking. Or, that there was plenty of land to be had. A couplet distributed by the London Company in 1630 tells of the dreams that were held out to immigrants:

> In England land scarce and labour plenty
> In Virginia land free and labour scarce.

Those who could pay their own fare across the ocean did, in fact, get 100 acres of land or more free—or at low cost. Those who couldn't, however, had to sell themselves into bondage for a given number of years to pay for the passage. Usually the period of slavery was four to seven years, but sometimes more. The captain of the ship would tear a contract into jagged halves, giving the emigrant one "indent" as a type of receipt, and keeping the other. Hence the term "indentured servant."

These people came willingly in search of a better life. But there were tens of thousands of others who came unwillingly. Some were kidnaped (the word comes from "kid nabbers") on the streets of London or the cities of the Continent. Some were criminals (often sentenced to death) sent here as slaves. They became known as "His Majesty's seven-year passengers"—because they would work as slaves for seven years and then be freed. Historian Richard B. Morris estimates that as many as 50,000 involuntary servants were brought to the Colonies, 20,000 of them to Maryland alone.

How many white slaves came, voluntarily or involuntarily, is a subject of dispute. But it is generally agreed that not less than a third and perhaps half of the 750,000 white immigrants during the colonial period were of this class.

The plight of these temporary slaves was unenviable. There was, to begin with, the passage. Ordinarily the trip lasted six to twelve weeks, but it might take longer. The average cargo was 300 people, but it was not unusual to have double that amount. The servants wore the same clothes throughout, lay flat for days when the small vessel was in heavy seas—sometimes next to a corpse—and went hungry or starved with painful frequency.

"There are many instances," writes historian James Truslow Adams, "where passengers almost fought for the bodies of rats and mice." On one ship carrying Scotch-Irish refugees, the "maddened passengers" ate six dead humans and were in the process of carving up a seventh when another ship came by and offered supplies. The number of dead was appalling. On one voyage of 400 Bavarians in 1709, 20 percent died. Of a cargo of 150 servants in 1730, only thirteen survived to see the new land. Another in 1745, with 400 Germans aboard, arrived with only 50 alive.

On arrival in America the indentured servant would be marched to the magistrate's office to take an oath to the king. Then he or she was put on the auction block. If there was no buyer, the shipmaster would turn the slave over to a "soul-driver" to be dragged through the countryside and offered for sale. Not infrequently, as with black slaves, families were broken up, children going to one master, the wife to another, and the husband to a third.

Since this was an age of few statistics, no survey exists on the ill treatment of indentured servants. But the subject comes up constantly in colonial accounts. The Virginia assembly noted in 1662 that "the barbarous usage of some servants by cruell masters bring soe much scandell and infamy to the country in generall that people who would willingly adventure themselves hither, are through feare thereof diverted. . . ."

Occasionally servants were beaten to death. There is the tale of Elizabeth Abbott of Virginia, who, after continual whippings, was found dead with "her flesh in some places . . . raw and very black and blew. . . ." Cases of inadequate food came to court over and over again. Servants ran away so often that Virginia passed a bill adding twice the time the white slave was gone to the term of service. A repeat of the offense was punishable by branding on cheek and shoulder.

Apart from the heavy work, inadequate food, and punishment, the white slave was restricted in his personal life as if in a prison. He could not buy or sell anything, or leave his master's home without permission. Marriage was prohibited, so that, as might be expected, bastardy became a frequent crime—all the more so since female servants were at the mercy of their masters. In 1663 fourteen cases of bastardy were tried in just one Virginia court.

It can be argued, of course, that white servitude was temporary, but four to seven years can be awfully long under such conditions. In not a few instances the indentured workers took measures against their plight. Some committed suicide. Some fled. Still others engaged in revolts. So great was their hostility that the colonial aristocracy was afraid to put guns in the hands of white slaves. When the governor of Virginia proposed military service for servants, he was turned down by the House of Burgesses on the grounds that the white slaves "might be tempted to obtain their freedom by slaying their masters."

Though the number of white slaves was large, it was not enough to keep up with the growing labor needs of the Colonies. Moreover, the indentured servant was relatively expensive. The cost of transport from Europe during the seventeenth century, plus commissions, ran to £12 per indenture. The cost of "freedom dues"—the food, clothing, tools, and sometimes a cow that the master was required to provide the servant at the end of bondage—came to another £10, for a total of £22. A young black, on the other hand, could be bought for £8 to £25 (by 1770, £50 to £80). He remained in bondage, however, not for seven years, but for life. He received no freedom dues, and what is more he produced children who were also slaves for life.

The colonists with increasing frequency turned, therefore, from white slavery to black slavery. The enslavement of Africans forms a special and gruesome chapter in the history of American poverty.

Black slavery was big business. In the century from 1686 to 1786 something like 2 million Africans were spirited away from the Black Continent, approximately 250,000 of them winding up on the American mainland. Connecticut, with only 30 black bondsmen in 1720, listed 6,500 in 1775. By the middle of the eighteenth century one out of every seven New Yorkers was black. The largest concentration, of course, was in the South, especially after the cultivation of rice and indigo was instituted. South Carolina had 32,000 black slaves in 1724, and 90,000 forty years later—approximately two-thirds of the total population.

The horror for black people began in Africa. English slave merchants made arrangements with African tribesmen to make war on other tribesmen and kidnap them. The unfortunate blacks thus kidnaped were then brought to the coast, sold, and transported overseas. Three black men and women died for every one who survived. Aboardship alone the loss was enormous. Of the 60,000 slaves sent to the Colonies by the Royal African Company from 1680 to 1688, 14,000 perished.

The change in lifestyle from Africa to America was so severe that nearly half of the blacks died within three or four years. After being sold on the auction block, they were treated to the usual infamies accorded men without rights. A Pennsylvania law of 1693 ordered that slaves "gadding about" be taken to jail, left without food or drink, and whipped with thirty-nine lashes. Runaway slaves in Virginia not infrequently had their ears nailed to the pillory and then cut off.

Suicide, flight, and revolt by the blacks were frequent. One mother, it is recorded, strangled every one of her thirteen chilmen, before taking her own life. A document advising planters how to handle would-be suicides noted that blacks sometimes "stifle themselves by drawing in the tongue so as to close the breathing passage, others take poison, or flee and perish of misery and hunger."

Occasionally the blacks rose in armed rebellion. Early on the morning of April 8, 1712, a group of slaves in New York City,

A *mutiny of slaves on an eighteenth-century slaver.* (The Bettmann Archive)

armed with knives, guns, and clubs, set fire to a house and waited for whites to cluster around it. Thereupon they killed nine and wounded seven. When they were captured six of the slaves committed suicide, twenty-one were hanged, burned, or broken on the wheel.

More serious was the revolt near Charleston, South Carolina, in September 1739. When the governor of Spanish Florida promised blacks freedom if they fled to his territory, a sizable band seized an arms magazine, killed its two guards, and moved westward toward the Edisto River. On the way, with colors flying and drums beating, they enrolled more slaves, shouted for liberty, and burned everything in their path. Thirty white men were killed. When the rebels were captured, seventy were hanged or gibbeted alive; ten were never accounted for. Perhaps they escaped to Florida.

All told, there were forty recorded revolts or conspiracies by slaves during the colonial period.

Slavery, black and white, was of course the worst form of poverty in colonial times. But there were others living in misery —tenant farmers, squatters, backwoodsmen. To be sure, Americans were better off than the people of Europe. Wages were 30 to 100 percent higher than in the old country. The ownership of land was also much more widespread.

The conflict between rich and poor was intense nonetheless. Merchants and large landholders became wealthier with each generation. There grew up in New England, for instance, a class of men known as the "River Gods" or "Lords of the Valley." Through political influence they were able to buy vast tracts of land for a song. Colonel Jacob Wendell of Boston bought 24,000 acres in western Massachusetts. Colonel Israel Williams of Hatfield held property in no less than a dozen towns. A prominent councilman of Boston and his partners were allowed to buy 106,000 acres in New England for the incredibly low price of £683.

In New York the situation was worse. The tract of the Van Rensselaers, near Albany, ran to 700,000 acres, that of the Van

Cortlandts 140,000, the Beekmans 240,000. Robert Livingston owned an estate sixteen miles long by twenty-four miles wide. One group of speculators, known as the "Little Nine Partners," secured a grant of a million acres.

In Maryland and the South, the trend was similar. Those with capital and political influence acquired massive estates. Thomas Berewood in 1731 was ceded 10,000 acres by the proprietor of the Maryland colony. At midcentury a man named Richard Bennet was the proud owner of a dozen plantations in Virginia and Maryland. When Robert Carter died in 1722, he left an estate of 300,000 acres and 1,000 slaves.

A group of favored Virginia gentlemen, including George Washington, were allocated 200,000 acres in the western part of the colony, with a pledge of another 300,000 if they would settle 100 families there within seven years. Holdings of 20,000 to 100,000 acres in South Carolina, while not commonplace, were not rare either. In North Carolina one group received 1,500,000 acres; another band of speculators, 500,000.

The inevitable consequence of such land accumulation was the emergence of a powerful land-owning class. That class was always in conflict with the tenant farmer, backwoodsman, and squatter. In 1751, for instance, tenants on the estate of Robert Livingston in New York refused to pay their rent, on the ground that they had been promised title to the land. An antirent revolt in Dutchess County, New York, involved 1,700 tenants. When it was suppressed, eighty were arrested, pilloried, fined. The leader, William Prendergast, was sentenced to be hanged, but no one could be found to act as executioner. To avoid further riots the governor pardoned him.

The poor tenants and small farmers felt themselves squeezed by high taxes, prices, and credit. Typical of how men became poor, even when they had access to land, is the story of the backwoods tobacco growers of Virginia. It begins with the Navigation Acts of 1660, in which English merchants were given a monopoly to buy the tobacco crop. In the next few years the price of the "noxious weed" was driven down by the monopolists from 3 pence a pound to a halfpenny a pound. At the same time

London traders raised the price of goods sold *to* the backwoodsmen—and the farmers fell into heavy debt. In the end the small planters organized a revolt, in 1676, that temporarily overthrew the government of Virginia. "The poverty of the country is such," said the leader of the rebellion, Nathaniel Bacon, "that all the power and sway is got into the hands of the rich, who by extortious advantages, having the common people in their debt, have always curbed and oppressed them in all manner of ways."

In a dozen different ways, then, colonial people succumbed to poverty. The misery of America was not like that of the Old World. But there were not a few who might have agreed with this anguished cry of an eighteenth-century Philadelphian:

> O these Liars. If I but had wings to fly, I would soon hie myself from hence to Europe, but I dread the tempestuous ocean and the pirates. . . . Whosoever is well off in Europe better remain there. Here is misery and distress, same as everywhere, and for certain persons and conditions incomparably more than in Europe.

The colonial leaders, like the leaders of England, did little to ameliorate the poverty of the slaves, or the poverty of the small farmer and tenant. The only part of the population for which they showed any concern was the helpless poor—the halt, the blind, the sick, the aged. The helpless were given relief much as in England under Queen Elizabeth's poor laws—and much as they are today.

Early records of Portsmouth, Rhode Island, that tell us of help given "ould John Mott" are perhaps typical. "Ould" Mott evidently was incapable of further labor, and his son, though willing to contribute a cow and corn for his father's support, had limited resources. The town therefore boarded Mott with a local citizen to whom it paid £9 annually for "diett and washing." The next year it voted to give Mott's caretaker 5 shillings a week "out of the tresurie . . . so farr as the tresurie will goe." In the next few years Portsmouth paid 40 bushels of corn to a Mr. Balston to take care of Mott's "home rome dyate lodging and

First debtor's prison in America—Williamsburg. (Colonial Williamsburg, Williamsburg, Virginia)

washings." Mott, it seems, was on the town's roll for thirteen years, and a constable regularly collected fees for his welfare. At one time it was decided to build a stone house for the old man's "more Comfortable beings."

The Elizabethan model was accepted as a matter of course in the New World. The Plymouth assembly passed a poor law in 1642, Virginia in 1646, Connecticut in 1673, Pennsylvania in 1688, Massachusetts in 1692. In New England taxes for poor relief were levied by selectmen or overseers; in the southern colonies the methods of collection varied. In New York the alderman in each ward prepared a list of needy, and the mayor provided for them out of the public treasury.

The simplest form of aid was the "putting out" system. A widowed lady in Hadley, Massachusetts, for example, was boarded with one freeholder after another for two-week periods. Ordinarily the putting out was for a whole year, with the selectmen paying for food and lodging, and the town providing medical care and clothing.

If the helpless were treated with some concern, however, the idlers were dealt with like ordinary criminals. According to the religious ideas of the time an able-bodied man who had no work was a "sinner" and was treated as such. He might be flogged, imprisoned, or bound out as a servant.

It was not unusual in Boston and other New England towns for able-bodied paupers to be sold at public auction for temporary servitude. Orphaned children, who were in danger of becoming idlers, were treated the same way. The courts of Chester County, Pennsylvania, in 1697 bound out thirty-three orphans for "service."

Where the punishment was neither servitude nor flogging, the culprits were clapped in jail—just as in the old country. Toward the end of the seventeenth and into the eighteenth century, it became too expensive to lodge idlers in prisons. Workhouses were therefore constructed, where the ne'er-do-wells were forced to labor for their keep. Connecticut had one such workhouse in operation by 1727, Boston by 1729.

3

The Holy Experiment

Once the gates of religious dissent had been opened in seventeenth-century England, some men began to question the social principles of the Church. Sects such as the Diggers and Levellers preached a Christian communism more characteristic of the Middle Ages. They interpreted literally the Biblical statement that "the poor shall inherit the earth."

A radical churchman, Gerard Winstanley, put forth a program to eliminate poverty by ensuring that "no man shall have any more land than he can labour himself . . . neither giving hire nor taking hire." Less extreme than Winstanley was a sect originally called Children of the Light, then Friends of Truth, and finally Society of Friends—but usually referred to as Quakers. Where the Christian communists urged total equality, the Quakers called on the rich to forgo all extravagance so that their surplus funds might be given to those less fortunate.

Other sects of course also spoke of concern for the poor, but no group in either England or America took this task so seriously. The abolition of poverty was for the Quakers a religious mission, God's word translated into practice. According to the Friends, every person had his personal relationship with God. That relationship was expressed in an Inner Light, guiding the individual toward self-development and love of his fellow man. Virtue, they said, could not be imposed on anyone from without —say, by priests or magistrates—but only from within, by his own conviction. Thus there was no need for big churches, paid clergymen, or sermons. Each man had his own access to God and in that sense was his own Christ.

The Quakers held meetings, not services, sitting in silence and communing with the Inner Light until constrained to share their concerns with others. They would not pay taxes to the Church of England, for to do so would concede the government's right to determine a man's religion. They would not bear arms or make war, for that was an abomination of the command-

Quakers going to meeting in 1776. (Library of Congress)

ment, "Thou shalt not kill." They would not swear an oath in court or on affidavit, since swearing was a blasphemy. They would not remove their hats for lord or king, since all men were equal before their Maker. They made decisions not by majority vote but by consensus: listening to everyone's views, until a "sense of the meeting" was arrived at.

The doctrine of the Inner Light had significant practical implications. If men communed with God in their own special way, society must be tolerant of all religious beliefs; and if they were all equal in the eyes of the Lord, they must also be equal before the law. This thesis, novel in the seventeenth century, imposed certain duties on the government, the foremost of which was to help citizens overcome poverty. "Let all the poor, the blind, the lame, and the crippled be cared for," read a Quaker pamphlet, "so that . . . you can claim to be the equals of the Jews; for they had the Law, which provided for widows, orphans, and strangers. Whoever closes his ear to the poor, closes it to the Law."

Among those who accepted the Quaker doctrine was William Penn, the eldest son of a distinguished English admiral. Tall, lithe, an excellent oarsman, a good swordsman, Penn was, in the words of historian John Fiske, "a picture of manly beauty, with great lustrous eyes under wide arching brows, a profusion of dark hair falling in curls upon his shoulders, a powerful chin, a refined and sensitive mouth." He was, in addition, as competent a scholar as an athlete. He spoke six languages fluently and was one of the most prolific writers of his time. His best known work, *No Cross, No Crown*, penned while imprisoned in the Tower of London, was a masterful argument against the established Church of England.

As sometimes happens with sons of the upper class, young Penn rebelled against the society in which his father had found such distinction. At the age of eleven, in 1655, he had a religious experience which led him to believe "that he had been awakened or called upon to a holy life."

Six years later, while at Christ Church, Oxford, Penn fell under the influence of dissenters, and either was expelled or was withdrawn from school by his irate father. For the next few years William studied law and theology, traveled in Europe, and might have become a typical patrician if he hadn't run into an old Quaker acquaintance, Thomas Loe. Loe taught him the principles of the Society of Friends.

Being a Quaker in the seventeenth century was akin to being a Communist nowadays, but far more dangerous. The Conventicle Act of 1664 made it a crime to worship God except through the Church of England, and many thousands were arrested for violating it. One day Penn was attending a meeting of dissenters when soldiers invaded the place and arrested those present. He was released from jail only after writing a note to a high official of his acquaintance.

Not many months later, however, Penn was again imprisoned, this time for writing a pamphlet which aroused the anger of the bishop of London. Even the son of a highly placed admiral was forced to remain in jail nine months for such an offense. In 1670, arrested once more for attending a meeting, Penn refused to take an oath of allegiance and was kept for six months in Newgate— the worst of English prisons.

Penn was not the only Quaker to suffer in England. According to a historian of Quakerism, at least 12,000 Quakers were jailed, and 300 died in prison.

Under such persecution the Friends sought relief in America. They settled in Massachusetts, Rhode Island, New York, Maryland, and Virginia, but except in Rhode Island they were treated badly. Two Quaker ladies, Mary Fisher and Ann Austin, who arrived in Boston in 1656, were jailed for five weeks and then deported to Barbados. When a few days later eight more Friends set foot in the city, they too were imprisoned. One Quaker, Mary Dyer, was twice sentenced to hanging. The first time she was reprieved with the rope already around her neck; when she ventured back to the colony a second time, she was hanged.

Penn, noting these developments from afar, determined to establish a Quaker colony in the New World. He was convinced that "governments, like clocks, go from the motions men give them. . . . Let men be good, and the government can not be bad;

if it be ill, they will cure it." All that was needed was a place where the Quakers could put this notion to the test of reality.

In 1680, then, Penn petitioned his father's friend, Charles II, for territory, still sparsely settled, "bounded on the east by the Delaware River, on the west limited as Maryland, and northward to extend as far as plantable." Since the king's family owed Sir William Penn's estate £16,000, the monarch assigned to the admiral's heir 55,000 square miles of fertile soil and rich minerals in lieu of the debt. Here, in 1681, the "second founder" of Quakerism founded "Pennsilvania," where he hoped to create a virtuous society of virtuous men.

William Penn's treaty with the Indians upon his founding of Pennsylvania in 1681. (Library of Congress)

Penn called his project the "Holy Experiment." It differed from other colonies in important aspects. Penn for instance refused to exaggerate about the prospects. "I shall say little in its praise," he wrote in a pamphlet inviting people to his domain. The land was sold or rented much as in other colonies—with two differences.

Pennsylvania (and Delaware, acquired by Penn from the Duke of York in 1682) was the only place in English America which opened its doors to all Christians. It did not go as far as inviting Jews or other non-Christians, but it gave refuge to more "foreigners"—Germans, Swedes, Finns, Dutchmen—than any other colony.

Pennsylvania was also far more liberal concerning the right to vote—even more liberal than Connecticut, the most democratic of the colonies at that time. Everywhere else a man had to own a certain amount of property and be of the right religion to vote. But in Pennsylvania those restrictions were so modest that ten times as many people had the franchise as back in England. For the small freeholder the ballot was an important protection against government abuse.

More directly affecting the common man was the code of laws. It was a common practice in those days to imprison those who could not pay their debts; Penn abolished imprisonment for small debts, though not for larger ones. The number of crimes for which the death sentence could be inflicted was reduced from the 150 in England to just 2—murder and treason. Prisoners, who formerly paid for their food and lodging while in jail, were relieved of that obligation, and steps were taken to separate criminals from the insane.

The jails themselves were transformed from abysmal dungeons where men vegetated, into workshops where an effort was made to rehabilitate them. Philadelphia prisons, according to visitors from Europe, were considered the least oppressive in the world. Philadelphia also had the most modern lunatic asylum in the Colonies, a fine hospital, and a reform school. Moreover, according to one writer, "no city in the world devoted a larger share of time and thought to philanthropic purposes."

In Penn's thinking, the poor were "the hands and feet of the rich . . . and to encourage them is to promote the real benefit of the public." At every meeting of the Quakers, therefore, help for the poor was one of the major items for discussion.

Men in difficult straits presented their problems to the group, or if embarrassed arranged for another member to report on their behalf. The meeting then voted sums for food, shelter, and coal, to be dispensed by a caretaker. Help was not confined to Quakers alone, but often included people who did not belong to the Society of Friends.

When a Friend was out of work, efforts were made to place him at a job, or if that was not possible to supply his family with raw materials to spin yarn at home. When a fire swept someone's home, money for rebuilding was made available through a special emergency fund.

In these and in other relief measures, what was unique was not only that aid was given, but that it was given by voluntary subscription. Every Quaker believed it a religious duty to give for the less fortunate, and he usually gave generously.

The Quaker concern for citizens began with childhood. Among the first laws passed in the colony was one requiring that children be taught to read and write by their twelfth year. Parents who failed to assure such education were fined £5. A year after Philadelphia was laid out, the community began building schools, both public and private, almost all of them coeducational. Such programs were many decades ahead of the times.

Both the sons of the poor and the sons of the rich were required to learn a trade so "that the poor may work to live, and the rich, if they become poor may not want." Concern for the individual ended with his funeral. If poor, he was buried with simplicity but dignity in the Quaker graveyard. Members of his Meeting, without distinction to status, were required to attend.

Concern is the key word for describing the Holy Experiment; it is a word that Quakers use to this day to express the Inner Light. It manifested itself not only in their dealings with one another but with the Indians and, to a lesser extent, with the blacks. Pennsylvania was not the only colony that paid the red man for his land; other colonies, notably New York, followed a similar practice. Historians are agreed, however, that Penn and his governors never practiced deception or debauchery. They neither plied the natives with drink nor drove a bargain to which they did not adhere.

The French philosopher Voltaire, alluding to one of the treaties between the Quakers and an Indian tribe, called it "the only treaty between savages and Christians that was never sworn to and that was never broken." During all the years that the Quakers ruled Pennsylvania and for decades afterward, they lived in peace with the Indians.

The Quaker approach to slavery was less exemplary, but by the standards of that period quite liberal. A community of German Quakers, headed by Penn's friend Francis Daniel Pastorius, petitioned the Yearly Meeting in 1688 to abolish slavery. It was an affront, they said, against the Biblical maxim, "Do unto others as ye would that they should do unto you." Pastorius denounced the kidnaping of blacks in Africa as un-Christian.

No action was taken by the Meeting, but five years later Friends were urged to buy slaves only for the purpose of freeing them, and to discourage with all their power further imports. Beginning in 1705 sterner measures were taken, and in 1711 a law was passed forbidding importation entirely. This law was unfortunately vetoed by the English monarch. A subsequent law three years later, imposing a prohibitive £20 duty for each black brought to the colony from abroad, was also rejected by the queen.

For all of its good points, the Holy Experiment did not succeed. To some degree it was due to Penn's long absence, which kept him in England for fifteen years. The men he left in charge were consumed with jealousies, as well as unqualified.

But there was more to it than that. As they became wealthier, Quakers forgot their original ideals. Some trafficked in slavery, despite the injunctions of the Yearly Meetings. The more prosperous began wearing fancy clothes and setting fancy tables.

Penn himself succumbed to high living. Though he urged moderation for others, he built a home worth £7,000. He wore costly wigs, set his table with silver dishes, rode in a luxurious cab, and operated an estate of 8,000 acres. He quarreled frequently with his tenants over the payment of rent. As Benjamin Franklin observed a long time later, he became "less of a man of God . . . and more of a man of the world." His sons, who were in charge of the colony after Penn's death in 1718, were even less "men of God." When the American revolutionaries confiscated their estate, it was found to be worth a million pounds.

With the growth of a lust for profit, the Holy Experiment disintegrated. Laws against unfair prices were violated. Lawlessness, never heretofore a serious problem, became more frequent; and criminal laws became more harsh—including such punishments as whipping, branding, mutilation. By 1767 the death sentence was being exacted for sixteen crimes, instead of two as originally.

Making money, rather than building the virtuous society, became the daily routine. Looking back at this period, members of the Society of Friends today say of their ancestors, "They came to America to do good—and did very well." Or, "They believed in 6 percent and God—in that order."

Apart from the Holy Experiment, the only other major attempt to build a "good society" during colonial times was the foundation of Georgia a half century later. In certain respects it was more liberal than the Quaker colony. It did not permit slavery within its borders. It accepted Jews and other non-Christians as equals. It operated on a nonprofit principle.

Georgia was colonized, however, for a unique reason.

Between South Carolina, which belonged to England; Florida, which belonged to Spain; and Louisiana, which belonged to France, was an uninhabited area. In 1715 the Yamassee Indians, encouraged by the Spaniards, had overrun part of South Carolina and killed hundreds of whites. The Yamassees in due course were defeated by Britain, but fear of Spanish designs ran high in London. To occupy the area between South Carolina and the possessions of the two other powers became, therefore, a powerful objective for empire-minded Englishmen.

One such man was James Edward Oglethorpe, a Member of Parliament for ten years and an ex-army officer who had fought with distinction against the Turks. Oglethorpe conceived the weird idea of mating Britain's security needs with the rehabilitation of criminals. Under an English law passed in 1717, judges were empowered to send convicts to the new world for seven years of servitude—"His Majesty's seven-year passengers"; or, if under a death sentence, for fourteen years. What Oglethorpe proposed was to bring them to Georgia as freemen, not as servants. In return, the former prisoner need only pledge that he would do military duty to defend the Crown's interests against Spain and France. Similarly, Oglethorpe sought to bring to his colony many small debtors who had recently been released from jail by Parliament, but who had no money and welcomed an opportunity to start over again elsewhere.

It was an alluring idea that seemed to give everyone what he wanted. In 1732 George II deeded to Oglethorpe and his associates a territory between the Altamaha and Savannah rivers, sea to sea, as a nonprofit colony. They were given absolute powers to enact all laws (subject to the king's veto), dispense justice, distribute land, raise funds, impose taxes.

No pretense was made at democracy. There was to be no voting or legislature. On the other hand, this was the only colony established that was neither a religious haven nor a means of making money.

Passage to the "land of liberty and plenty" was paid for by the philanthropists out of funds supplied by Parliament and private subscription. Once in Georgia—appropriately named after the king—the ex-convict would work on a community farm for a year. After that he would be given free a plot of fifty acres, plus a sixty-by-ninety-foot lot in town on which to build a home. Not only land, but food, clothing, and tools were his for the asking.

To make sure that enough people came, the trustees of Georgia also appealed to nonconvicts in Germany, Switzerland,

Scotland, and elsewhere, on somewhat different terms. Anyone bringing ten servants with him was allotted 500 acres; the servants themselves, after four years of bondage, were to be given 20-acre holdings. No one was to be excluded on grounds of religion except Catholics, who were deemed unreliable for any war against Catholic Spain. For the same reason, Oglethorpe prohibited not only black slaves but free blacks.

Hopes ran high as Governor Oglethorpe sailed with 130 carefully screened persons in the autumn of 1732. The warm climate, it was believed, was perfect for producing a silk to rival Italian silks. It was expected that the production of this commodity would give work, part time and full time, to 40,000 people. The prospect for growing grapes on "the finest land on all the continent" and developing a wine industry also seemed favorable.

But the trustees and Oglethorpe had seriously miscalculated the land's potential. Georgia, it soon became apparent, was not the place for either silkworms or grapes, and the planting of rice —soon to become its main product—was difficult because of the hot climate and malaria. Instead of tens of thousands, then, less than 2,500 ex-convicts could be lured to the "future Eden," and many of them either died or fled northward to South Carolina. The fifty-acre plots for the former prisoners and the twenty-acre holdings for freed servants proved inadequate for anyone to eke out even a minimal living.

As of 1741 Georgia numbered only 1,500 to 2,000 people. A report to the trustees complained that "the colony is reduced to one-sixth of its former number. . . . The few who remain are in a starving and despicable condition." An attempt was made to liberalize conditions for the settlers by increasing grants for ex-servants to fifty acres and by lifting restriction on the sale of land. But it was a losing battle. Georgia could not survive on the design set out by Oglethorpe. It soon was steeped in all the vices Oglethorpe had sought to avoid.

Before long, the sale of rum to Indians, carefully prohibited originally, was legalized. Slavery was introduced in 1749, and six years later a slave code was promulgated that was as extreme as any in the southern colonies. It provided, among other things, for entering slave homes without warrants, and for punishment of the black man with impunity. Instead of basing itself on convicts and philanthropy, the colony now invited large landowners from South Carolina and England.

By 1751 the original venture was a shambles. Georgia reverted to the Crown as a royal colony on a model unintended by Oglethorpe. Rice production, slavery, and large plantations became its dominant characteristics; the liberation of the poor and the rehabilitation of criminals, a vague memory.

4

After the Revolution

"Not worth a continental!"

During the American Revolution that began in 1776, the Continental Congress issued paper money which people referred to as "continentals." Theoretically the old English pound was worth 5 American dollars. But the new money kept falling in value because there was no gold, silver, or anything else of value behind it. Thus a bowl of toddy in Virginia sold for $1 in silver coins, but cost $500 in paper continentals. In 1781 a pair of stockings sold in Philadelphia for $300, tea for $90 a pound. The best way to call something worthless was to say it was "not worth a continental."

The runaway inflation of the revolutionary period caused much hardship. Many a patriot was forced to sell his farm, many a family went hungry. "Not a day passes my head," an army officer reported, "but some soldier with tears in his eyes hands me a letter to read from his wife. . . . [The letter says] 'I am without bread, and cannot get any . . . we have no wood, neither can we get any. Pray come home.' "

The common man was saddled with debts. According to a leading historian, one half of Vermont "was totally bankrupt, the other half plunged into the depths of poverty." A similar story could be told for most of the former colonies. The same historian says that if the laws for imprisonment for debt had been enforced in New Hampshire in 1785, almost two-thirds of the people would have been in jail. There was such suffering during the critical years of 1783–88 that some former revolutionaries took arms against the government. The worst such revolt, in Massachusetts, was led by Captain Daniel Shays in 1786. Two thousand insurgents invaded the courts to stop their farms from being foreclosed—sold to pay the due mortgage. They burned barns and seized property belonging to the rich, and held parts of the state for months before they were subdued. They were not opposed to the Revolution—most had fought in its army. But they felt that while they had been making sacrifices, the speculators were making money—and the profiteers had grown rich on their labors.

Despite all this, however, the American Revolution prepared the way for one of the most important attacks on poverty in the history of the country.

One of the major results of the Revolution was the acquisition of land by many who had none.

In November 1777 the Continental Congress suggested to all states that they seize the property of those who supported the king of England. This proposal was greeted with enthusiasm everywhere except in South Carolina. Of the large landowners, 29 lost their estates in New Hampshire, 490 in Pennsylvania, 55 in New York.

Massachusetts took every acre of those who fought for Britain, including the holdings of the Pepperell family, which ran thirty miles along the coast. Pennsylvania grabbed the farms of the William Penn family, valued at $5 million (1 million old British pounds), and paid the family $650,000. New York confiscated the 300-square-mile manor of the Philipse family, the land of the De Lanceys, and other holdings totaling about half the acreage in the state. New Jersey seized 500 large Tory farms. Virginia commandeered the 6-million-acre Fairfax estate. The

American rebels also took land belonging to the king and the proprietors, who owned the charters for former colonies.

All this land was sold by the thirteen states for much-needed revenue. In the process, however, the big farms were divided into tracts suitable for the small and middle-sized farmer. Thus James De Lancey's estate was broken up into 275 separate farms, that of Roger Morris into 250. In a single year New York put 5½ million acres on the auction block for a few quarters an acre.

The result, of course, was that many land-hungry tenants or artisans were given a chance to acquire their own land.

The Revolution also dealt kindly with another section of the poor—the squatters. Families living on previously unused land, which technically belonged to others, were offered the right to preempt that land at generous terms. In Virginia, squatters were permitted to keep 400 acres each, provided they agreed to plant corn for a year. A law of 1781 allowed squatters to buy land at $5 a hundred acres—payable in two and a half years.

Still another boon to those without land were the bounties that had been given to lure men into the army. Virginia in 1779, for instance, gave 300 acres plus $400 to each volunteer.

The most significant result of the Revolution, both for the poor and for the nation, was the opening up of the territory west of the Appalachians. Beyond the watershed, from West Florida to the Great Lakes and from the Alleghenies to the Mississippi, was 488,248 square miles of land—as against 341,752 square miles of the original states.

It is painful to speculate what might have happened to the fledgling nation if this real estate had not fallen into its hands. Britain had prohibited its colonists to settle beyond the Appalachians, and it held onto the "west" during the Revolution. But Britain was also worried that its great rivals, Spain and France, might take the territory. At the Treaty of Paris, therefore, it ceded the area to the United States.

Even so, there were hurdles to overcome before the west could be opened. There were the Indians, who had a rightful claim to "Indian Country," and who resisted the American advance in scores of little wars. And, of course, there were the problems of nature.

But the west filled out far more quickly than most American leaders had expected. By 1783 there were already 25,000 settlers there—the largest number in Kentucky, where revolutionary soldiers had been given land warrants by Virginia. And once the war was over, the rush became a tidal wave. Hardy families by the thousands moved over Wilderness Road or down the Ohio River into Kentucky. By 1790 Kentucky boasted a population of 74,000 and was about to enter the union as a state. Tennessee had 35,000. The year Marietta, Ohio, was laid out—1788—some 10,000 people passed through it.

Had the thirteen states followed European precedent, they might have made this region a colony—or colonies. But in the Ordinance of 1787 three to five territories were scheduled to be carved out of the area. When any of them had as many as 60,000 eligible voters, it had the right to become a state "on an equal footing with all others." Slavery was outlawed in what was then called the northwest.

The big question concerning the northwest was not land itself but how to distribute it. Alexander Hamilton, leader of the conservatives, proposed that it be sold in large tracts that only wealthier people could buy. Thomas Jefferson, leader of the radicals, at first favored giving it away, then swung around to a less extreme position. He insisted it be sold in small plots at low cost.

The final policy, contained in the Land Ordinance of 1785, was a compromise—but closer to Hamilton's views than Jefferson's. The government would lay out rectangular communities (townships) thirty-six miles square. One thirty-sixth of each township was to be put aside for public schooling. For the rest, one half was to be sold at auction, at a minimum of $1 an acre (later $2), and the other half in sections one mile square. This favored the land-jobbers (speculators) because 640 acres cost $1,280—considerably beyond the means of the average citizen.

Under relentless pressure, however, Congress in 1800 reduced the size of land for sale to parcels of 320 acres; in 1804 to 160 acres; and in 1820 to 80 acres. Moreover, some ingenious souls found ways around the law. Each township was to be surveyed before being put up for sale—but some families simply settled beyond the territory surveyed. Before Congress's program got under way there were already 7,000 squatters in unsurveyed territory. Many more were to follow. And though the government sometimes used troops to evict squatters, it was also forced to pass preemption acts periodically which permitted the squatter to gain title to the land at so much an acre.

There were many speculators who grew rich in the west by a

Plowing of the prairies beyond the Mississippi. (Library of Congress)

variety of means. Nonetheless, the opening of the west reduced poverty appreciably, and deepened the democratic spirit. By 1790 some 221,000 pioneers lived in the sprawling paradise beyond the Appalachians.

"The practical liberty of America," wrote an Englishman in 1817, "is found in its great space and small population. Good land, dog-cheap everywhere, and for nothing if you will go for it, gives as much elbow room to every man as he chooses to take. . . . They come, they toil, they prosper. This is the real liberty of America."

Apart from reforms relating to land ownership, the revolutionary nation liberalized voters' rights, modified imprisonment for debt, and struck a few modest blows against slavery.

Restrictions on the ballot had never been so severe in the Colonies as in England. Yet in each of the Thirteen Colonies a man had to own a certain amount of property to vote; and if he wanted to run for office, considerably more. Benjamin Franklin once told the delightful story of a man who had the precious right to cast a ballot because he owned a mule. But when the mule died, his right perished with it. "I wonder," mused Franklin, "who had the vote, the man or the mule?"

In Massachusetts wealth of $300 was needed to cast a ballot, $500 to $1,000 to run for Congress, $1,500 to $3,000 to become a senator, and $5,000 to stand for governor. As late as 1790, only one man in ten could vote in New York City.

Yet, in irregular fashion, there were soon many changes for the better. Pennsylvania's constitution of 1776 granted the ballot to any male who paid taxes. Delaware, North Carolina, and New Hampshire followed suit. Pennsylvania also passed laws giving all free men the right to hold public office regardless of wealth or religion.

Another matter in which there was some improvement was relief for the debtor. Originally a man could be thrown in jail for owing someone a few dollars, and while in jail be forced to pay his own upkeep. As late as 1785, even in Philadelphia, half of the inmates of prisons were debtors. New York jails in 1787–88

housed 1,200 men unable to pay obligations, which were sometimes as small as $5.

In 1789, New York passed a law limiting imprisonment to
thirty days if the debt was less than $50. A Pennsylvania bill in
1792 required that creditors pay part of the upkeep for imprisoned
defaulters. Following the Shays Rebellion in Massachusetts, a
law was enacted granting freedom to debtors who swore they
had no money to pay their bills. Imprisonment for debt was not
finally eliminated until a half century later, but it was relaxed in
some places after the Revolution.

Another cry heard from revolutionaries—also relating to poverty
—was for emancipation of the slaves. Jefferson, though he did
not free his own slaves because they were pledged as security for
his debts, called for full emancipation. So, too, Patrick Henry and
George Washington. Thomas Paine, the great pamphleteer of the
Revolution, urged that the slave be not only freed but given a
generous gift of land.

The demand for emancipation, as might be expected, was
strongest in those states which had little to lose. Vermont's constitution of 1777 prohibited the enslavement of anyone "born in
this country or brought from over sea." But Vermont had few
slaves within its borders. At the time of the Revolution there were
4,000 black bondsmen in Rhode Island, 5,000 in Massachusetts,
6,000 each in Pennsylvania and Connecticut—as against 200,000
in Virginia and 100,000 in South Carolina. Obviously it was
less painful to the pocketbook to free 4,000 pieces of property than
100,000. Abolition of slavery therefore was limited to the North.

Laws for gradual abolition were passed in Pennsylvania in
1780, Connecticut and Rhode Island in 1784. In Massachusetts
the task was accomplished when judges ruled that the words
"free and equal" in the Constitution applied to all men, regardless of color. In ruling against an owner who beat his slave,
Chief Justice William Cushing held that the "idea of slavery is
inconsistent with our own conduct and Constitution." By 1804,
when New Jersey agreed to gradual emancipation, all states
above the Mason-Dixon line were free territory.

Another type of poverty, that of the indentured servant, passed from the scene entirely. With blacks available in large numbers, southern planters lost interest in white servants.

By haphazard steps, then, the founding fathers developed an impressive antipoverty program inherent in the principles of revolution. Unfortunately, however, while poverty was being eliminated for some people, the industrial revolution was soon plunging—and keeping—many others in dire distress.

5

Bitter Fruit

In 1789, the year Washington became President, a "smuggler" arrived from England. Samuel Slater, barely twenty-one, was not smuggling diamonds or marijuana, but a plan for a labor-saving machine. The reason he had to smuggle it was that Britain prohibited either the export of machinery or drawings of machinery. Artisans who worked on machines were barred from leaving the country, for fear they would disclose industrial secrets. As the leading manufacturing nation on earth, Britain didn't want other nations to catch up with it. Hence the stern measures.

Young Slater, an employee of an English factory, had read an advertisement by a Pennsylvania society offering $500 for improvements in textile machinery. Obviously he couldn't take such machines with him, nor could he hide blueprints on his person or in his luggage. But he could carry out with him the plans in his head. Disguising himself as a farm boy, Slater made his way to London, then to New York. With the help of an American Quaker he established a cotton mill in Pawtucket, Rhode Island, where he built water frames and spinning and carding machines from the plans he had "smuggled" out. Nine small children tended the factory.

Slater is considered by many historians to be the "father" of American manufacture.

Not everyone was enthusiastic about labor-saving machinery. Secretary of State Thomas Jefferson felt that America should remain a nation of small landholders. He had seen the factory system at work in England and France, and he was convinced it would rob laborers of independence and force them to work at low wages. He also was distressed by the employment of women and small children for such long hours, at backbreaking jobs. Though he later changed his mind, Jefferson's initial reaction to the factory system was hostile.

Alexander Hamilton, Secretary of the Treasury, a handsome redhead born in the West Indies, took the opposite position. Yes, it was true that four-sevenths of the workers in British mills were women and children. But by working, he said, they were "rendered more useful . . . than they would otherwise be." The factory system, he argued, would give the "rich and well-born" greater power—and it was the rich and well-born, in his opinion, who should rule a country. In addition, manufacture would encourage immigration and help populate the United States.

The onrush of manufacture, of course, could not be slowed. The machine saved time and produced mountains of goods. In the following decades, stimulated by the War of 1812 during which British manufactured goods were not available, the factory system spread wings like a great eagle.

By 1830 there were 795 cotton mills in the United States, valued at $45 million; by 1860 there were 1,091, worth more than double that amount, employing 122,000 laborers. On the eve of the Civil War, 140,000 industrial establishments were in operation, with a capital of more than a billion dollars and employing 1.3 million workers.

The industrial revolution was not just a minor addition to American life. It changed virtually everything.

When Washington became President, 90 percent of the people lived in villages. There were only six cities with more than 8,000 population. When Lincoln became President, there were 5 million

View of the Boott Cotton Mills at Lowell, Massachusetts. (Library of Congress)

people in a total of 141 cities. Manhattan alone had 813,669, Philadelphia 566,000, Baltimore 212,000.

The destination of the immigrant in colonial days—whether he was an independent landowner, a tenant, or an indentured servant—was the farm, the rural scene. But with the industrial revolution twice as many came to the cities as to the villages. Labor was needed not only for the factories, warehouses, and stores, but for building turnpikes, digging canal beds, and eventually for laying ties for the railroads. Since labor, as usual, was in short supply it had to be imported from Europe.

Immigration, therefore, increased dramatically. It was about

5,000 a year in Washington's day; 100,000 in the year 1842; 427,833 in 1854. In New York, St. Louis, Chicago, and other cities, half the residents were foreign-born.

City life, the immigrants found, was very much different from farm life. The farmer planned his crop, grew it, and marketed it his own way. He made the major decisions. The laborer on a construction project or in a factory, on the other hand, was ordered about by others. Decisions were made for him by foremen and bosses.

In a sense the city laborer was more free. He could move

Landing from an immigrant ship in 1851. (Library of Congress)

around from one place to another. He could work or not work, as he pleased—idleness was no longer punishable by imprisonment or flogging. But if he couldn't find a job, he starved. And his life was much more insecure than on the farm. No matter how bad times were, the villager always had a few potatoes in the barn, chickens to lay eggs, a cow to give milk. He could somehow survive. But the city worker, unless he had money in the bank or went on charity, was in a more precarious situation. Time and again during economic slumps he faced actual hunger. He had to live off relatives or scrounge for food on a soupline.

During the 1819 depression a jobless man in Philadelphia wrote, "This year the question is how to exist." He meant it literally. A study by a research committee showed that employment in thirty Philadelphia industries had fallen from 9,672 in 1816 to 2,137 in 1819—and total wages from $58,000 to $12,000.

A report from Cincinnati at about the same time described "distress as beyond conception." Many who had no money to buy wood faced the prospect of freezing. Newspapers pleaded for clothing to give them some protection from the cold. Some people left for the backwoods to grow food for themselves.

After the industrial revolution got under way, depressions occurred once a decade, sometimes more often—and almost no one could tell when they were coming. One day all was well; the next, disaster struck.

The panic of 1837, for instance, was a shattering event. With only a brief interruption in 1842–43, it lasted for eight long years. Six hundred banks closed their doors in a single year. At one time nine-tenths of the factories in New England were out of operation. One-third of the laboring class was idle, and wages for the rest fell 30 to 50 percent. In New York alone, 200,000 city people lived "in utter and hopeless distress with no means of surviving the winter but those provided by charity." This was the time when Horace Greeley urged the jobless to "fly, scatter through the country, go to the Great West, anything but stay here."

If the industrial revolution, then, greatly increased the produc-

Run on a savings bank during a financial panic. (Library of Congress)

tion of goods, it also piled a new and more wretched type of poverty on top of the others.

The new, urban poverty, like the older forms of poverty in America, centered around the immigrant. When the immigrant landed in New York (or Boston, or wherever), a "runner" boarded his ship to try and rent him a room in a boardinghouse. Invariably the rental was three or four times the normal rate. Other runners—Irishmen for the Irish, Germans for the German—offered him a job hundreds of miles away. The runner made all sort of promises about good conditions and high wages, but it never turned out that way.

Once settled, the immigrant found himself the object of criticism and scorn. He was accused of "stealing" jobs from native workingmen. Thus Mayor Aaron Clark of New York, elected on the Native American ticket in 1837, told the city council that immigrants "necessarily drive our native workmen into exile. . . ." The immigrant, he said, "will bring disease among us; and if they have it not with them on arrival, they may generate a plague by collecting in crowds within small tenements and foul hovels."

In point of fact, the immigrant worked for low wages not because he wanted to replace a native, but because he could not do better. Far from being a conspirator against others, he was victim of a thousand greeds.

One of the most debilitating features of his life was the slum he lived in. As the cities saturated with people, it became a sellers' market for those who had apartments to rent. Building owners converted single-family houses into two, three, and four tiny apartments. When such converted buildings proved insufficient to accommodate the need, multistory tenements rose that were just as bad or worse—overcrowded, lacking ventilation or sunlight except in the front and back rooms, shoddily constructed, ridden with disease and crime.

A Lowell, Massachusetts, citizen reported in 1847 that in one small tenement apartment "I found one of the families to consist of a man, his wife and eight children . . . and four adult boarders. . . . This by no means furnishes the worst case." In the Irish-German Tenth Ward of New York, the density of inhabitants per acre grew from 54.5 persons in 1820 to 171 just twenty years later.

When the buildings were full, people rented the cellars. The chief of police of New York in 1850 noted that one out of every twenty people inhabited cellars, the average per room being six people. In one cellar there were twenty per room. According to a labor historian, the life expectancy of an Irishman after he moved into the Boston slums was fourteen years.

"In these places," said Horace Greeley, "garbage steams its poison in the sun . . . thieves and prostitutes congregate . . . disease lurks. . . ." Tuberculosis, cholera, typhoid, pneumonia, and scrofula were particularly widespread, taking their heaviest toll of children under five.

Horace Greeley. (Library of Congress)

Water usually had to be drawn from outside hydrants. Privies were behind the building. The "contents, instead of being drained or carried away, frequently overflowed to the surface and created breeding places of disease." As late as 1857 only 138 miles of sewer had been laid in New York City's 500 miles of streets, and conditions in other cities were worse.

If the slum was the gathering place of city poverty, its source was the wage system. Because of the shortage of labor, except in depression times American wages were better than those of England or Europe generally. Yet in the absence of trade unions, living standards for the unskilled were near the destitution level.

In March 1851 Horace Greeley published an estimate of what a family of five would need as a minimum budget. The figure, $10.57 a week, included food, clothing, fuel, and rent, but only 25 cents for wear and tear on furniture and 12 cents for the daily newspaper—nothing else. Yet, to Greeley's dismay, not one of nine crafts in the iron and steel industry averaged $10.57 a week. The common laborer was paid 89 cents a day, just half the minimum budget.

"I ask," wrote Greeley, "have I made the workingman's comfort too high? Where is the money to pay for amusements, for ice cream, puddings, trips on Sunday up or down the river, in order to get some fresh air; to pay for the doctor or apothecary, to pay for pew rent in the church, to purchase books, musical instruments?"

In Massachusetts at midcentury men earned about $5 a week, women about $2, and children, who constituted 40 percent of the work force, 50 cents plus board. Top wage for a female worker in Philadelphia was $1.50, out of which she paid 50 cents for lodging plus additional money for wood. The workday averaged twelve and a half hours in 1830; eleven hours thirty years later.

It was not unusual, then, to hear the free laborer's plight compared to that of the slave. "A common slave in the states of Virginia, Tennessee and Kentucky," charged one minister, "is much better compensated for his labor by his necessary food, clothing, lodging and medicines, than many respectable workers and daughters in this city [Philadelphia]. . . ."

A large number of workers in the first half of the nineteenth century were Irish. Laboring on the toughest jobs, such as canals and turnpikes (later the railroads and the mines), they were the most exploited people in the country—next to the blacks. Thousands of them traveled hundreds of miles to work at digging a canal—for 62½, 75, 87½ cents a day, out of which they paid

From the Old to the New World. Above: *Irish emigrants leaving their homes for America.* Below: *German emigrants embarking on a Hamburg steamer. (Library of Congress)*

$1.50 or $2 a week board. Working in marshy land under terrible conditions, they often returned to their families with ruined health and almost no money. "Hundreds are swept off annually, many of them leaving numerous and helpless families," wrote a liberal businessman about their plight. Those working on turnpikes earned less—50 to 75 cents a day, "exposed to the broiling sun in summer, and all the inclemency of our severe winters."

The lot of working children in the nineteenth century was particularly appalling. Their hours were long and they had little opportunity to go to school. A labor paper in Philadelphia reported in 1830 that no more than one-sixth of the boys and girls in cotton mills "are capable of reading or writing their own name." But six-, seven-, and ten-year-old children were forced to work because the parents needed their earnings to survive.

There were thousands of abandoned, orphaned, or runaway youngsters in the country. A New York police report of 1852 indicated that 10,000 children in that city alone were living on the streets, sleeping in privies, hallways, or on barges—anyplace where their little bodies could fit.

The advance of industry affected everything, including home life. Innumerable homes were converted into miniature factories. Much of the manufacture in the nineteenth as well as the early twentieth centuries was performed in households on a contract system, especially in the needle industries. Businessman Matthew Carey described a room on 11th Street in Philadelphia, fifteen feet by eleven, where two couples and four children lived and did home work. One woman spooled, the other spun; between them they earned 20 to 25 cents a day. But since both husbands had been unemployed for weeks, it was the only income for eight people.

In another such home a charitable organization found the Mc-Giffie family, with the father emaciated, the mother "lying in a state of insensibility—one child . . . dead, the other dying." Not all home workers, naturally, were in this extreme condition, yet the home work system with all its vices and tragedies was a familiar feature of American life until two generations ago.

Native-born Americans generally fared better than immigrants, skilled workers better than the unskilled. A craftsman earned $7 to $10 a week in the 1830's, enough to maintain a decent standard —particularly if one of the children was working. Even so, large numbers of people were unable to stay out of debt.

The fruit of city life and industrialism, at least in the beginning, was affluence for some, but increased pauperism for many. "Thirty years ago," wrote the labor reformer George Henry Evans, in 1844, "the number of paupers in the whole United States was estimated at 29,166, or one in three hundred. The pauperism of New York City now amounts to 51,600, or one in every seven of the population."

6

Reform, Charity,
and Temperance

In answer to the poverty of the cities, concerned men and women began to form trade unions as far back as the 1790's, to fight for higher wages and shorter hours. They also organized the Working Men's parties—popularly called "Workies"—to win certain reforms. From 1828 to 1834 sixty-one such parties were formed. Workingmen who went to the polls to elect a mayor in New York in 1834 sang this song which expressed their sentiments:

> Mechanics, cartmen, laborers
> Must form a close connection,
> And show the rich Aristocrats,
> Their powers at this election.

In addition there were many utopian schemes put into practice by reformers. In 1825 Robert Owen established a utopian community in Indiana called New Harmony. The idea was to share things in common. Later, other utopian communities sprang up under the leadership of Albert Brisbane and Horace Greeley. There was also the famous Brook Farm, which included among its supporters such renowned figures as Nathaniel Hawthorne, George Ripley, Margaret Fuller, and Ralph Waldo Emerson.

What distinguished the unions, Workies, and utopian communities was the emphasis on *collective* action. The downtrodden would help themselves through their own forms of protest. The leaders of these movements were either radicals who believed in revolution, or reformers who proposed to change things more slowly. Through their efforts—and through liberal government officials—the average man in America won a number of significant improvements in this period.

The fourteen states that joined the union from 1789 to 1840, for instance, granted the right to vote to all male whites, without any requirement that they own land or be of a certain religion. Gradually, too, property and religious qualifications were eliminated in the original thirteen states as well.

Another change related to the penal codes. Flogging, the pillory, branding, cropping of ears, were abolished in favor of fines or imprisonment.

A more significant reform was the elimination finally of imprisonment for debt. This was a major hardship for many thousands of people. In 1816, for instance, there were 2,000 New Yorkers in jail for debt; one man had been there three years, another six. A man in Vermont was imprisoned for owing 54 cents to two creditors; another in Philadelphia for owing 2 cents. Beginning in the 1820's, but especially in the 1830's, one state after another passed laws to end this inhumane practice.

Certainly one of the most important achievements of this period was the inch-by-inch advance toward a free, compulsory education system. It took a bit of doing, for while people favored education, they didn't want to pay the taxes needed to build and operate schools.

Under the prodding of such men as Horace Mann of Massachusetts and Henry Barnard of Connecticut, however, the public was finally convinced that it must invest in a crusade against ignorance. The first steps toward compulsory education were timid: state and municipal grants to existing religious and private schools. Then laws were enacted requiring communities to levy taxes for education. Finally came the cancellation of tuition fees, the establishment of teacher training schools, and laws making it mandatory for all children to have at least a few years of schooling.

Despite such changes in the democratic process, however, the government felt it had only a limited obligation to the poor. It operated on Adam Smith's doctrine of *laissez-faire*—leave alone. The poor, like the rich, were to be left alone to make their own way. Thus the only changes in the old Elizabethan system of poor relief were those made necessary by the growth of poverty, rather than the result of any new ideas on the subject.

The main method of relief in the past, when life was almost entirely rural, had been home relief. Overseers of the poor provided money and necessities to the indigent either in their own homes or in the homes of others. But home relief was now inadequate. More and more, then, the poor in need were placed in almshouses, or put out on "contract" or "auction." The advantage of the almshouse (or "poor farm," as it was called) was that the pauper could perform a little work, such as spinning, cooking, picking fruit, or farming, thereby keeping costs down. The well-operated poor farm at Poughkeepsie, New York, boasted that it spent only $25 a year—50 cents a week—for the upkeep of each of its inmates.

The almshouse was a place where society could pack its poor out of sight and out of mind. Whatever the original motives for building them, the trend was usually toward overcrowding and neglect. Reformers throughout the nineteenth century complained of the bad food, the intermingling of sexes and ages, filth, and other vices to which a system of this kind lent itself. The Boston House of Industry in 1834 reported a hundred children, some only infants, as well as sixty insane among its population.

Another means of dealing with the helpless poor was the contract system. The community placed its needy in the care of householders at a specified weekly, monthly, or annual fee. The town of Beekman in Dutchess County, New York, paid $32 annually for each person farmed out who was over twelve, and $16 for each child below that age. One farmer in Amsterdam agreed to accept all the town's idle for a flat fee of $350 a year.

Written agreements with the contractors spelled out areas of responsibility. For instance, a local undertaker contracted with the town of Fitchburg, Massachusetts, "to Board, Clothe and Comfortably provide for, in sickness and health the persons hereafter named. . . ." If any died the town was to bury them, or, if sick, the town was to pay the doctor's bills. The undertaker was "to have the benefit of the labor of said Paupers, and receive his pay quarterly."

Under the auction system a man, woman, or child was placed on the block, much as slaves used to be, and auctioned off to the person willing to accept the lowest amount for his care—in return also, of course, for his labor. The bidder himself was sometimes only a notch or two above that of the men he "bought," so that in an indirect way he was relieving his own misery.

Again, corruption and neglect were almost invariable by-products of such an arrangement. "Notwithstanding the large amount raised in this county, for the support of the poor," charged a respectable citizen of Westchester County, New York, "they are neither fed, clothed, nor treated like human beings. . . . Most of the parish poor are now sold, as the term is . . . to those who agree to support them on the lowest terms . . . [and] who treat them in many instances more like brutes than like human beings. . . ."

In due course humanitarian pressures forced modification of many of these practices. The increase in orphanages, insane asylums, and houses of correction took people from the almshouses and jails to institutions better suited for their problems. The sale of paupers was curtailed, and more almshouses and poor farms were built. But essentially, poor relief was little altered from what it had been a century before.

What did change was the scale and character of private charity. Philadelphia, with a population of 130,000 in 1829, listed thirty-one institutions dealing with human misfortune. There were the Provident Society for employing the poor, an orphan society, an association for the care of "Coloured Orphans," an "Indigent Widows and Single Women's Society," the City Infant

School Society, the Institution for the Deaf and Dumb, the Society for Alleviating the Miseries of Public Prisons, and so on.

To radicals, such as Ralph Waldo Emerson and Henry David Thoreau, these "do-gooders" or "bleeding-hearts" were wealthy people who were salving their own consciences for having robbed the poor in the first place. Thoreau made fun of "a charity which dispenses the crumbs that fall from its overloaded tables. . . ." There was nothing particularly generous, he felt, about men who gave to charity 5 or 10 percent of their earnings while keeping the rest of their ill-gotten gains.

But among the philanthropists were some who in their own way considered themselves the true benefactors of the lower classes.

Typical of such men was Thomas Eddy, one of sixteen children born to Quaker parents in Philadelphia. Eddy had helped the British during the American Revolution. After the Revolution he prospered in the insurance business, and then as a land speculator. "In this business," he writes, "I made a good deal of money." Rich and a man of substance, he now decided to do good for the less fortunate.

Like his fellow philanthropists, Eddy was a mixture of compassion and self-righteousness. He was opposed to horse racing and liquor because they were a "source of vice and criminality." He joined the New York Bible Society because he believed that Bible reading would help the poor overcome their moral weakness. But he also built a fairly modern prison for the state of New York, opened a savings bank (then a novelty), administered a hospital, helped establish an insane asylum and a free school for poor children, organized a reformatory for juveniles, and gave considerable aid to Indians.

Eddy's major achievement was the founding in 1817 of the Society for the Prevention of Pauperism. The purpose of the society was to investigate the "circumstances and habits of the poor" so as to devise "means for improving their situation."

According to the society there were ten causes of poverty. High on the list were ignorance, idleness, liquor, and hasty marriage. Men were also poor, said the society, because they refused to save money, played the lotteries, did business with pawnbrokers, and visited houses of prostitution. Relief given by charities, the society held, did only temporary good; in the long term it was harmful because it made the man or woman less self-reliant.

Clearly, according to the philanthropists, it was the poor person's own fault that he was poor. It was his own weakness and sinfulness that caused his plight. And the way to catapult him out of his poverty was to give him "friendly" advice on how to live a life without drink, gambling, or similar temptations. Eddy's society proposed to set up a savings bank, suppress street begging, encourage churchgoing, close liquor shops, and supply materials for labor at home.

Robert M. Hartley, best known of the philanthropists before the Civil War, founded the New York Association for Improving the Conditions of the Poor (AICP) in 1843. It adhered in the main to the same principles as Eddy's society. The first of Hartley's stern beliefs was that relief was due the impoverished as a *favor*, not as a right. The second was that indiscriminate aid pampered the needy and therefore contributed to their indigence. The third was that private charity was preferable to public relief.

During the depression which began in 1854, the AICP criticized city relief committees because they committed such "indefensible indiscretions" as urging the poor not to pay rent. The opening of soup kitchens was denounced on the principle that "the poor should not be aided in promiscuous masses . . . but by personal visits at their homes." In the twelve months ending November 1, 1855, the AICP people visited 15,549 families and doled out $95,018 in aid—a large operation at the time. But it was done solely on an individual basis, and as a favor.

One of the most sustained crusades allegedly aimed at relieving poverty was one against the "Demon Rum." The crusaders at their peak numbered a million zealots, and were able to enact prohibition laws or local option bills in Maine, New York, Vermont, Rhode Island, Michigan, Connecticut, New Hampshire, Tennessee, Delaware, Illinois, Indiana, Iowa, Wisconsin, and the territory of Minnesota.

That many people spent their last penny on the Demon Rum,

STEP 5.
The summit atta[...]
Jolly compani[...]
A confirmed drun[...]

STEP 4.
Drunk
and
riotous.

STEP 3.
A glass
too
much.

STEP 2.
A glass to
keep the
cold out.

STEP 1.
A glass
with
a Friend.

leaving nothing for their families' rent or groceries, was of course a well-known fact. City prisons overflowed with such drunkards, who sometimes constituted a majority of the inmates. The question was what to do about people of this type.

In colonial days courts sometimes tried to shame drunkards by requiring them to wear the letter D on their clothes. After the Revolution the Continental Congress urged states to make illegal "the pernicious practice of distilling grain." Dr. Benjamin Rush, a friend of Thomas Jefferson's, wrote a book about the effects of

STEP 6.
*Poverty
and
Disease.*

STEP 7.
*Forsaken
by
Friends.*

STEP 8.
*Desperation
and
crime.*

STEP 9.
*Death
by
suicide.*

The drunkard's progress, from the first glass to the grave. (Library of Congress)

liquor on the body and mind that eventually sold 172,000 copies. Liquor, he said, was not harmful when taken on occasion, but it had evil effects on novices or those who drank habitually. The early temperance movement, following Rush's principles, campaigned for self-control rather than total abstinence.

But early in the nineteenth century, temperance became associated with religious revivalism and turned more extreme. Leaders of the Congregational and Methodist churches, and men such as the Rev. Lyman Beecher were "teetotalers"—opposed to drinking at any time, even occasionally. Beecher compared liquor to slavery, as "sinful, impolitic, and dishonorable." He and his friends called for a massive boycott of stores and hotels that sold ardent spirits. By 1829 there were 1,000 local societies with 100,000 members crusading against liquor; five years later there were 5,000 groups with 1 million adherents.

The movement foundered for a while in the 1830's, but was revived in 1840 when a group of six friends who frequented a Baltimore tavern took the temperance pledge and later formed the Washington Temperance Society. The new society had no religious character; it was solely a movement of reformed drinkers to reform others who drank. As such it succeeded beyond all expectations. Three years after being organized it reported, probably with some exaggeration, that half a million drinkers had taken the pledge.

Everywhere the temperance people, like true evangelists, held parades and demonstrations. With children in the front lines, wearing satin badges, they sang the stanzas of "The Cold Water Army" and signed a pledge that ran as follows:

> We do not think
> We'll ever drink
> Whiskey or Gin,
> Brandy or Rum,
>   or anything
> That'll make drunk come.

The agitation by these groups eventually brought about political changes. Almost all states introduced bills to license liquor dealers. Massachusetts outlawed the sale of retail liquor in any amount less than fifteen gallons—obviously an impossible hurdle for the common man.

In 1846 Maine became the first state to prohibit the manufacture or sale of liquor entirely. Thirteen other states followed suit.

Fortunately or unfortunately, however, enforcement was lax,

except in Maine, New Hampshire, and Vermont. The Civil War drew the nation's attention to other matters and ended the temperance crusade—temporarily. By this time a counterreaction had set in. Many influential people argued that government supervision of private habits was an encroachment on liberty. The Maine law, they said, was unconstitutional.

At any rate there is no convincing proof that the temperance crusade reduced poverty to any measurable extent. The causes of poverty seemed to lie deeper than the Demon Rum.

7

"Vote Yourself a Farm"

Residents of New York City woke one morning in March 1845 to find walls plastered with a circular that bore the intriguing headline: "Vote Yourself a Farm."

Are you an American citizen [ran the text]? Then you are a joint owner of the public lands. Why not take enough of your property to provide yourself a Home? Why not Vote yourself a farm? . . .

Are you a party follower? Then you have long enough employed your vote to benefit scheming office-seekers; use it for once to benefit yourself. Vote yourself a farm.

Are you tired of slavery—of drudging for others—of poverty and its attendant miseries? Then, Vote yourself a farm. . . .

The circular was a reprint from a radical sheet, *Working Man's Advocate,* available at ten for a penny, and eventually sold by the hundreds of thousands. Editor and publisher of the *Advocate* was a man of pleasant face, symmetric features, a beard that stretched around the chin, and thin but wide lips. His name— George Henry Evans. In his time Evans had advocated other plans for rescuing the workingman from his misery. But this one was to leave its mark.

Born in Herefordshire, England, in 1805, Evans was brought to the New World and apprenticed at the age of fourteen to a printer in Ithaca, New York. Print shops those days seem to have been schools for radicals, perhaps because they were good places to do some reading. Evans read the works of radicals like Tom Paine and, in the words of his brother, emerged "a firm and consistent infidel." After roaming about for a while Evans came to New York City late in 1829—just in time to help build the first labor parties.

The Working Men's Party of New York had begun at a mass meeting of 5,000 laborers to protest an increase of the workday from ten hours to eleven. Following a quick victory, the workers turned their thoughts from the ten-hour day to political action—just as was happening in Philadelphia and dozens of other cities. The Workie formed in New York was led by a self-educated machinist, Thomas Skidmore, who held the view that there was no cure for man's misfortunes unless property were equally divided.

Skidmore urged the government to give every man over twenty-one and every unmarried woman 160 acres of land free of charge, to be held as long as he or she tilled the soil. Selling or renting land would be illegal. Anyone who currently owned more than 160 acres would keep it, but it would pass to the government after his death. Thus within a single generation, according to Skidmore, everyone would be truly equal, as provided for in the Declaration of Independence.

Evans at first spurned Skidmore. Instead he made common cause with the two leaders who opposed Skidmore—Robert Dale Owen and Frances ("Fanny") Wright, a beautiful redheaded woman who was considered the most dangerous radical of her time. The Free Enquirers, as this group was called, proposed to establish tax-supported boarding schools in which children of the rich and those of the poor would be brought up together. They would be taken from home at the age ·of two. Living in conditions of full equality, they would eventually grow up and transform the nation in their own image. Or, at least, that was what Owen and Fanny expected; the Free Enquirers' plan was never tested.

After the Workies disappeared, Evans changed his political position, borrowing liberally from Skidmore. He was now convinced that third parties were of little value—that labor should work within the two major parties, putting forth its own candidates only as a last resort. He also concluded that poverty would always exist unless workingmen could escape to the public domain. "The poor," he wrote, "must work or starve in the manufactories as in England, unless they can cultivate the land."

After six years working a forty-acre farm in New Jersey, Evans returned to the big city to promote his "vote yourself a farm" plan.

The 1840's were a time of worsening conditions for the poor. Immigration rose by 300 percent, from 600,000 in the previous decade to 1,700,000. And with the expansion in number came an expansion of misery.

Dr. Henry Clark reported visiting a building on Half-Moon Place in Boston with three cellar apartments. One of them was occupied each night by no fewer than thirty-nine persons. In another the "tide had risen so high that it was necessary to approach the bedside of a patient by means of a plank which was laid from one stool to another; while the dead body of an infant was actually sailing about the room in its coffin."

A doctor in Lowell, Massachusetts, compared factory work to jail. Slaves in Richmond's tobacco factories worked ten hours a day, but Lowell's free workers toiled twelve hours ordinarily, and thirteen and a half hours in April. Girls in these plants were forced to live on company premises, crowded six to a room "of moderate dimensions"—not any better than the average jail.

Revulsion against the factory system in England had once led to a wave of machine-breaking. Around 1811, armed bands descended on Nottingham mills in the dark of night to destroy the hated labor-saving devices. In land-rich America the same revulsion resulted in back-to-the-farm movements. It was an idea that had occurred to Jefferson and Skidmore, to Robert Owen, and to

New England factory life. Above: *Bell time (drawing by Winslow Homer).* Below: *A skirt factory. (Library of Congress)*

Albert Brisbane, Horace Greeley, Henry James, Nathaniel Hawthorne, Emerson, Margaret Fuller, Bronson Alcott, George Ripley, to name a few—who sponsored thirty-four utopian communities in the 1840's.

George Henry Evans' new agrarianism was in the same tradition, a retread in fact of the ideas of Skidmore, Tom Paine, and others. Its saving grace was that it was more effective. "If any man has a right on the earth," Evans wrote in his magazine *Radical*, "he has a right to land enough to raise a habitation on. If he has a right to live, he has a right to land enough for his subsistence."

The reason wages were low, said Evans, was that the worker was forced to remain in the city. Speculators had seized the public lands, making them too expensive for the urban dweller to buy. Hence there was a "surplus of mechanics" in the city. Supply was greater than demand, and wages, as a consequence, were held to a mere subsistence level.

The way to get around the frauds of the landjobbers, Evans argued, was for the government to give its lands to the people— free. Many city workers would then flee to the rural areas, causing a shortage of labor in the cities. With demand greater than supply, wages would go up to a decent level. Thus, land reform would help not only the man who fled to the farm but the one who remained in the factory as well.

On a Sunday in February 1844, Evans called together five friends in a room behind John Windt's print shop in New York. The group formally launched the National Reform Association. The scheme they elaborated had the merit of simplicity. The federal government would lay out, in the public domain, "rural republican townships" six miles square, each subdivided into 144 quarter sections of 160 acres each.

Every landless person willing to settle and work a quarter section would receive it free of charge. It would be inalienable; that is, it could not be sold, rented, or put up as security for debt. There was enough land in "the possession of the general government," said the National Reform Association, "to allow every family in the United States two hundred acres each, besides all the land now held in private property in the twenty-six States and Territories."

Evans' plan was not hard to sell. It could be compressed into that single attractive slogan, "Vote Yourself a Farm." By September 1845 national reform groups were functioning in twelve New York counties and six or eight states. The *New York Courier and Enquirer* called the plan "wild," "utterly senseless," "fatal to society," "thoroughly destructive to all social and civil interests." But it won converts in high places. Gerrit Smith, a philanthropist and landowner, became a spokesman for the National Reformers in Congress.

The most important convert was Horace Greeley, publisher of the most widely read periodical of the time, the *New York Tribune*—and one of the most colorful figures in American history. At one time or another Greeley had spoken out for a dozen causes, including the abolition of capital punishment. On meeting Evans, he became an advocate of National Reform. Greeley wrote:

Make the Public Lands free in quarter-sections to Actual Settlers and deny them to all others, and earth's landless millions will no longer be orphans and mendicants. . . . When employment fails or wages are inadequate, they may pack up and strike westward to enter upon the possession and culture of their own lands on the banks of the Wisconsin, the Des Moines or the Platte, which have been patiently awaiting their advent since creation. Strikes to stand still will be glaringly absurd when every citizen is offered the alternative to work for others or for himself, as to him shall seem most advantageous.

With Greeley and others agitating for National Reform, Evans could set about to make it a political reality. Each Democratic or Whig candidate was asked to write a statement endorsing land reform; and if he did, he was given the full support of the "vote yourself a farm" movement. On the other side, every applicant for membership in the National Reform Association had to commit himself not to vote for anyone who did not make such a pledge.

With a small but growing legion behind him, Evans could sometimes produce enough votes to be a balance of power between the two major parties. Thus he also was able to win a sympathetic ear from candidates for office. Only where there was no candidate friendly to their movement did the land reformers occasionally run their own—usually with poor results.

Evans was also shrewd enough to hitch his star to other popular causes. The New England Working Men's Association had been formed around the single issue of winning the ten-hour day. The National Reformers joined with it to call industrial congresses, which met annually from 1845 to 1856 and attracted quite a few trade unions. Through this amalgamation Evans also gained access to the prominent Brook Farm writers. He joined hands with the antirent groups in Albany County, New York; with Thomas H. Dorr's People's Party in Rhode Island (formed to secure manhood suffrage); and with the antislavery movements of Michigan, Wisconsin, Indiana, and Massachusetts. Though Evans had reservations about most of these causes, he was flexible enough to blend them with his own. National Reform, he wrote in 1846, initiated an era in which there "will be but two parties, the great Republican Party of Progress and the little Tory Party of Holdbacks."

No one was as yet thinking of a "Republican Party," but many National Reformers were prominent figures in forming that party during the next decade. By a dozen different routes the program for free, inalienable, and limited homesteads insinuated itself into the bloodstream of the Republican Party. Future President Andrew Johnson introduced a homestead bill in Congress in 1846, and Horace Greeley introduced one two years later.

Galusha Grow, called by some the "father of the Republican Party," made his first important speech in Congress in 1852 on the subject, "Man's Right to the Soil." The Vermont convention of the Republican Party in 1854 came out for free grants of land to actual settlers, and the Pennsylvania Whigs, when they shifted to the Republicans, hoisted banners reading: "Free Men, Free Labor, and Free Land."

Evans was four years dead when the Republicans held their Chicago convention in 1860. But William H. Seward, one of the leading contenders for the presidential nomination, had been a pioneer supporter of land reform; and Abraham Lincoln was also considered favorable to the idea.

Two years later, when the Republicans came to power, they made it the law of the land—one of the most important pieces of legislation in the nation's history, the Homestead Act.

But the Homestead Act embodied only one of Evans' three principles: free land to the man who settled it. The other two

The farmer pays for all. (Library of Congress)

principles, nonalienation and equality, fell by the boards. The idea that no one be permitted to sell, rent, or mortgage his quarter section was dropped as too radical. In typical political compromise, the Republicans moved simultaneously in both directions. They gave homesteads to many poor but gave much larger grants to the rich. As an inducement to build more trackage, the railroads were allotted vast domains—free. And speculators were able to gobble up millions of acres from the public domain by a variety of techniques.

The National Labor Union at its 1867 convention in Chicago, just five years after the homestead bill was enacted, noted with dismay the trend toward speculation:

> The course of our legislation recently has tended to the building up of greater monopolies. . . . Eight hundred millions of acres of the people's lands have been legislated into the hands of a few hundred individuals, who already assume a haughty and insolent tone and bearing towards the people and government. . . . These lands are held unimproved, and mainly for speculative purposes. . . .

By 1890, twenty-eight years after the Homestead Act was passed, some 48 million of the billion acres in the public domain had been given to 372,659 families—about 2 million people. But in the same period the nation's population grew by 20 million. Moreover, the railroads, with the aid of bribed congressmen, got four times as much land as the 372,659 families combined. Three western carriers chartered between 1862 and 1864 were awarded not only federal loans for each mile of track they laid but outright gifts of 70 million acres.

What had begun as a radical doctrine to achieve equality ended as a reform with enough loopholes for any landjobber to crawl through. Evans had elaborated a timetable that would have the United States by 1900 a "Nation of Freeholders," without a trace of poverty. But while the Homestead Act did bring benefits to millions, it fell far short of the objectives foreseen by the man who had formulated the idea. In any event it had only a minor effect in diminishing poverty.

8

"No More Dat!"

There exists no more disheartening chapter in the history of poverty than that of the miscarried efforts of black Americans to win freedom. The Civil War freed them from bondage, but they have yet to win economic or political equality.

It is ironic that this should be so, because southern whites had more reason to be on the side of the blacks than on that of the plantation owners. The poor white had little or no stake in slavery; indeed, the enslavement of the black man hurt him too.

As of 1860 there were 4 million slaves and 8 million whites in the fifteen slave states. At least three-quarters of the 1½ to 2 million white families owned no slaves at all. Of the 384,000 that did, the vast majority had between one and ten. Only 10,781 plantation owners possessed as many as fifty slaves, and only 1,733 a hundred or more.

Less than one percent of the southern white population lived like blueblooded aristocrats. But the poor whites, with no slaves or just a few, usually tilled inferior land and eked out a bare livelihood.

William Gregg of the South Carolina Institute stated in 1851 that nearly half that state's 274,563 whites were "substantially idle and unproductive, and would seem to have sunk into a con-

Discovery of Nat Turner, leader of a slave revolt in 1831. (Library of Congress)

dition but little removed from barbarism." Many lived "an existence but one step in advance of the Indian of the forest." They survived by hunting, fishing, a little trade in slaves, occasional

jobs, or minor thievery. Sometimes, said Gregg, they entered
into league with black men to steal together.

The slave economy retarded the development of almost everything except cotton. Some manufacturing did come to the South,
but it was small-scaled and employed slaves or else whites who
were paid much less than they would have received in the North.
At a time when men in the factories of Lowell, Massachusetts,
were earning 80 cents a day, similar workers in Tennessee were
receiving 50 cents. Women in Lowell were paid $2 a week; in the
South, $1.25. In North Carolina, factory labor—either slaves
rented to industrialists by their masters, or free whites—cost $110
to $120 a year; according to a writer who lived there, it would
cost "at least twice that sum in New England."

The mass of southerners clearly had nothing to gain from
slavery. In the long run, even the large plantation owners might
have been better off without it. The price of a slave kept going
up, especially after the traffic with Africa was cut off in 1808.
Slaves were now bred for sale in old tobacco states such as
Virginia—and they were more costly.

A prime field hand in Georgia cost $300 in 1792, $1,000 in 1819,
$1,200 in 1853, and $1,800 on the eve of the Civil War. To this
must be added interest on capital, taxes (since the slave was
property just like a textile spindle), insurance (against death,
illness, injury, or flight), as well as a modest upkeep.

The northern capitalist paid his workers weekly wages, nothing
more. His surplus money was put into labor-saving machines. The
southern plantation owner had so much capital tied up in his
laborer (the slave) that he was always in debt to his banker and
so had little left for improving the land or buying machinery.
Many students of the subject believe he would have been better
off freeing his slaves and rehiring them at a daily wage. The
initial loss would have been great, but the long-term benefits
much greater.

The slaveowners, however, had become wedded to their way of
life. Sensitive and intelligent individuals defended slavery as
morally superior to the "wage slavery" in the North.

"The difference between us," boomed Senator James H. Hammond of South Carolina, "is that our slaves are hired for life and well compensated; there is no starvation, no begging, no want of employment among our people. . . . Yours are hired by the day, not cared for, and scantily compensated, which may be proved in the most deplorable manner, at any hour in any street of your large towns."

Defenders of the system gave innumerable instances where slaveowners were more humane than northern capitalists. Francis Scott Key of Maryland explained to a friend that he was pro-slavery because he "could not, without the greatest inhumanity be otherwise. I own, for instance, an old slave, who has done no work for me for years. I pay his board and other expenses, and cannot believe that I sin in doing so."

When a canal was dug through the swamps of Louisiana to Lake Pontchartrain in 1835, it was necessary to import hundreds of Irishmen because slaveowners would not hire out their blacks for the work. It would, they said, endanger the slaves' lives. Dr. Richard Arnold, during the cholera epidemic of 1849, wrote to a friend: "I wish an Abolitionist could see the care and attention bestowed upon our Negroes. . . . A manufacturing cotton lord can easily fill the place of his dead operative and he loses nothing by his death. A planter loses so much capital by the death of every one of his operatives, and hence to save his capital is to save his Negroes."

On the plantation where Booker T. Washington was born in Franklin County, Virginia, the master and his sons worked side by side with the six slaves. "In this way we all grew up together, very much like members of one big family. . . ," wrote Washington. According to this famous ex-slave, "On some of the large estates in Alabama and Mississippi . . . master and slaves frequently lived together under conditions that were genuinely patriarchal."

Though it was illegal to teach a black how to read and write, not a few masters did, and some gave special instruction in higher education to young blacks of talent. A slaveowner named John McDonough introduced in 1825 a system of self-government for his slaves, including trial by a jury of peers. Jefferson Davis is said to have copied this design for his two farms in Mississippi.

A master in North Carolina was noted for feeding his slaves exactly what his own family ate, housing them in well-built bungalows, providing them with "plenty of firewood . . . good shoes and ample clothing." When sick, the chattels were attended by the best physicians in the area. Ailing children were taken to the master's home and treated with the same care as his own youngsters. Every adult black man was given a "patch of ground" to cultivate for himself, and time to work it.

The record of slavery is not one solid mass of brutality. Some servants, it is true, were worked to death within six or seven years; but these were exceptions, not the rule. Others were sold away from their families, never to see wife or children again. On the other hand, many lived with kith and kin by their side till the end of their days.

A slave auction in the South. (Library of Congress)

Some black men were given assignments of responsibility, such as foreman, "head of the culinary department," or a similar post. Some were permitted to earn cash by working on holidays, Sundays, and nights cutting wood, blacksmithing, selling produce. There were not a few instances where owners took their bondsmen north in order to free them. As of 1860 there were 262,000 free blacks in the South, one for every sixteen slaves— and that year another 3,018 were emancipated.

Clearly there was no uniformity to the slave system; it was diverse enough that one could find testimony for any point of view.

When the balance sheet is drawn, however, the chattel slave lived in the most demeaning poverty the nation has ever known. Whatever apology is made for slavery, the fact is that the slave, no matter how hard or zealously he worked, could seldom raise his living standard beyond the level of bare necessity.

If there were a few who subsisted on the same diet as their masters, the vast majority tasted little but corn meal and bacon or salt pork. "All that is allowed," reported an ex-slave, "is corn and bacon, which is given out at the corncrib and smoke-house every Sunday morning. Each one receives, as his weekly allowance, three and a half pounds of bacon, and corn enough to make a peck of meal." On thousands of plantations the slave seldom, if ever, tasted beef, milk, fruit, eggs, or fresh vegetables.

The typical shelter—"quarters"—was a cabin of crudely cut, loose-fitting clapboard without lining, "so that only the thickness of a single board kept out the winter's air and cold."

"Small, low, tight and filthy, their houses can be but laboratories of disease," wrote an Alabama physician. Often there were no windows; roofs leaked; chimneys, made of mud and wood, disintegrated.

There were exceptions, of course, but on the other hand there were conditions so mean as to be barbaric—such as a certain Georgia plantation where the slaves were given neither chairs, tables, plates, knives, nor forks. According to Kenneth M. Stampp, "They sat . . . on the earth or doorsteps, and ate out of their little cedar tubs or an iron pot, some few with broken iron spoons, more with pieces of wood, and all the children with their fingers."

As for clothing, apart from hand-me-downs given to house servants, the typical ration was a few yards of "Negro cloth" such as calico or linsey-woolsey, one or two pairs of pants a year, a woolen jacket, a pair of shoes. Frederick Douglass in his autobiography says that he "was kept almost in a state of nudity," as a child, "no shoes, no stockings, no jacket, no trousers; nothing but coarse sack-cloth or tow-linen, made into a sort of shirt reaching down to my knees. This I wore night and day, changing it once a week."

The tyranny of the system is indicated by the cost of upkeep. Stampp lists records of a number of plantation owners showing "that the yearly charge for the support of an adult slave seldom exceeded $35.00 and was often considerably less than this." On Edwin Ruffin's plantation in Virginia the cost of upkeep for each slave was only $25 a year; on that of James Hamilton, it averaged $18.33 over a forty-year period. James A. Tait of Alabama estimated his annual expenses, including food, clothing, medical care, and taxes, as $34.70 for each chattel; and Thomas Pugh of Louisiana at $23.60.

Worst of all was the insecurity of slaves, even those who belonged to the most kindly of masters. No story can be as heartrending as that told by a reporter for the *New York Daily Tribune* (March 9, 1859). It described the auction of 436 men, women, children, and infants of the Major Butler estate. The auction took place at the racecourse near Savannah, Georgia. None of the blacks had ever been sold before, but now that the Major was dead his sons had decided to get rid of the estate, including, of course, its most valuable property, the slaves.

As the auction approached, every hotel in Savannah was jammed by the speculators, who had come from as far away as Virginia and Louisiana, lured "by the prospect of making good bargains." The black families huddled at the racecourse for a week or more in pitiful anxiety over their fate. Would they be separated from their spouses, their children, their parents, the

Sale of estates, pictures, and slaves in the Rotunda, New Orleans. (Library of Congress)

persons they loved? The Butlers had promised that they would be sold "in families," but a family was considered to be a man and wife.

As the speculators lit cigars and consulted their catalogues, the Negroes were examined with as little consideration as if they had been brutes indeed; the buyers pulling their mouths open to see their teeth, pinching their limbs to find how muscular they were, walking them up and down to detect any signs of lameness, making them stoop and bend in different ways that they might be certain there was no concealed rupture or wound; and in addition to all this treatment, asking them scores of questions relative to their qualifications.

The reporter overheard Elisha, chattel No. 5 in the catalogue, trying to convince a "benevolent looking middle-aged gentleman" to

purchase him, with his wife, boy and girl, Molly, Israel and Sevanda, chattels Nos. 6, 7, 8. The earnestness with which the poor fellow pressed his suit, knowing, as he did, that perhaps the happiness of his whole life depended on his success, was interesting, and the arguments he used were most pathetic.

With all his passion Elisha tried to show that his was a hard-working family that should be purchased as a whole:

"Sho' you won't find a better man den me; no better on de whole plantation; not a bit old yet; do mo' work den ever; do carpenter work, too, little; better buy me, Mas'r; I'se be good servant, Mas'r. Molly, too, my wife, Sa fus rate rice hand; mos as good as me. Stan' out yer, Molly, and let the gen'lm'n see."

When the sale was over—it brought $303,850—Mr. Pierce M. Butler, now of Philadelphia, gave each black as he or she was led away a gift of four 25-cent pieces. That ended the Butler family's responsibility.

No wonder, then, that President Lincoln's Emancipation Proclamation brought so much joy to millions of black people. As of January 1, 1863, according to the President's decree, all slaves in the rebel states were to be "then, thence forward, and forever free."

A happy black expressed the sentiments of all at a meeting in Washington the day before the proclamation was to go into effect:

Onst the time was dat I cried all night. . . . De nex mornin my child was to be sold, and she was sold, and I neber spec to see her no more till de day ob judgment. Now, no more dat! no more dat! no more dat! Wid my hands agin my breast I

was gwine to my work, when de overseer used to whip me
along. Now, no more dat! no more dat! no more dat! . . .
We'se free now, bress de Lord. Dey can't sell my wife and
child no more, bress de Lord! No more dat! no more dat! no
more dat, now! Preserdum Lincum have shot de gate!

Black people were soon to learn, unfortunately, that to be free
of bondage was not to be free of poverty.

9

Forty Acres and a Mule

Unscrambling the slave system, after two and a half centuries, was no simple matter.

To begin with, many Americans did not believe it possible—or desirable—to incorporate blacks into the white man's culture. Blacks, they felt, should be colonized elsewhere—out of sight and out of mind. Even so dedicated an abolitionist as that slender Quaker Benjamin Lundy suggested that slaves be freed only "gradually," and then be sent to Haiti, Texas, or Canada. Abraham Lincoln, too, favored colonization. His friend and adviser, Francis Preston Blair, proposed in November 1864 that "a portion of Texas on the Rio Grande" be put aside as "a refuge for the freedmen of the South to go to. . . ." When Congress freed the slaves of the District of Columbia in April 1862, it allocated $100,000 to find a home for them somewhere else.

Most northern leaders opposed slavery as an institution, but they had no strong feelings about the black man or woman as a human being. Despite the fact, for instance, that the North and West had long since abolished slavery, only six states granted black men the right to vote. New York required that a black own $250 in property to vote. Ohio granted the right only to mulattoes —with more white blood than black.

The Civil War, contrary to popular notion, was not fought to

Campaign poster for the election of 1860. (Library of Congress)

free the slave but to "preserve the Union." When Lincoln was inaugurated on March 4, 1861, he said, "I have no purpose . . . to interfere with the institution of slavery in the states where it exists. I believe I have no right to do so, and I have no inclination to do so." During the war, when General John C. Frémont ordered some slaves freed in Missouri, Lincoln revoked the order. The 900 blacks who fled to the camp of Major General Benjamin F. Butler were not freed but declared "contrabands of war"—property—to be disposed of later.

The Crittenden Resolution passed by Congress after the North lost the first battle at Bull Run reassured the five loyal slave states —Delaware, Kentucky, Maryland, West Virginia, and Missouri —that slavery would not be touched within their borders. Ultimately, it was practical considerations that caused Lincoln to free the slaves. The black was the backbone of the southern economy. He and his wife and his children grew its food and cotton, built the military earthworks, drove the horses, and did the other menial jobs, without which the Confederate army could not function. To win away the slave from his master was therefore an intelligent way to weaken the enemy. The promise of freedom was made, in large measure, for that purpose.

In stages, then, the chattels were liberated. Congress freed those in Washington, D.C., in April 1862, and those in the territories belonging to the United States two months later. In July, the Administration offered freedom to "any man or boy of African descent," as well as to his mother, wife, or children, who rendered service to the Union—such as spying. In September, finally, Lincoln issued his Emancipation Proclamation, abolishing slavery in eleven rebel states—when and if they were occupied by federal troops.

It was a grand act that stirred great hopes in the black community. But there were some abolitionists whose enthusiasm was restrained. The former chattels had relied on their masters for food, shelter, and clothing. How would they now fend for themselves? Where would they get the money to start life over again, to buy land, a mule, a few implements? No provision was made for such things. "That proclamation," said Wendell Phillips, "frees the slave but ignores the Negro."

For the next decade and a half this subject was a source of concern for friends of the black people, as well as the blacks themselves.

No man tried harder to help the former chattels solve their economic problems than the congressman from Lancaster, Pennsylvania, Thaddeus Stevens. He was called by his biographer "the most powerful parliamentary leader our system of government has ever evolved." Until his death in 1868 he certainly had more influence in Washington than President Andrew Johnson. It was Stevens and his friends who impeached Johnson and who came within one vote of having him removed from office. Yet even with such power, Stevens failed to carry legislation to give every black family "forty acres and a mule."

Thaddeus Stevens.
(photograph by Mathew
Brady, Library of Congress)

The "Old Commoner," as Stevens was called, got along tolerably well with Lincoln. But he disagreed strongly with the President about preserving the Union at all costs, even if that meant continuation of slavery. After the Civil War began, Stevens proposed to Lincoln that he arm the blacks, arrest southern leaders, seize their lands, send them into exile, and execute some of them. Stevens wanted the South utterly defeated; Lincoln wanted reconciliation. This division between Lincoln and the radical Republicans—Stevens and Senators "Bluff Ben" Wade, Zachariah Chandler, Charles Sumner, and others—was deep and enduring.

With the assassination of Lincoln in April 1865, the conflict between the radical Republicans and the new President, Andrew Johnson, became sharper. Johnson, a former tailor from Tennessee, followed what was called a restorationist policy. He tried to restore the white southern leadership to all or most of its former power. Under him 14,000 Confederate gentry, including General Robert E. Lee, had their plantations returned or were compensated for those destroyed. By January 1866 white administrations were back in office everywhere in the South except Texas, and many Confederate leaders had been reelected to the United States Congress.

Thus restored, the southern aristocracy passed "Black Codes" aimed at keeping the blacks "in their place." A black was required to carry his labor contract on his person at all times or be jailed for "vagrancy." In Mississippi, if he were without "visible means of support" he could be imprisoned or sold into servitude for a specified period, to pay off a fine. In Alabama he could be put to work under state overseers. In Maryland a freedman convicted of minor crime could be placed in bondage for years.

Special laws set wages and hours of work for ex-slaves, and imposed prison terms for those who left the plantation before their employment contract had expired. South Carolina set a fee of $10 to $100 a year for a black man or woman who sought work at anything but agriculture and domestic service. The effect was to return ex-slaves to their old masters. In some places the law provided that blacks could come to town only with permission of their employers.

A bill in Mississippi, ironically called an "Act to Confer Civil Rights on Freedmen and for other purposes," forbade intermarriage between whites and blacks, restricted the renting of lands or homes, barred blacks from carrying firearms or drinking liquor, and restored all the old laws not specifically rescinded. The whip and the pillory came back into general use. Planters organized terrorist groups such as the Black Cavalry, a predecessor of the Ku Klux Klan, to keep the ex-slave subdued.

"The rebellion has not ceased," Wendell Phillips exclaimed, "it has only changed its weapons. Once it fought, now it intrigues;

once it followed Lee in arms, now it follows President Johnson in guile and chicanery; once its headquarters were in Richmond, now it encamps in the White House."

The gulf between Andrew Johnson and Thaddeus Stevens was as wide as the labels they used to define their policies—"restoration" versus "conquered provinces." Where the one would restore the Confederate aristocracy to power, the other would not only destroy it but seize its land so that it would never rise again. Where the one would withdraw federal troops, the other would retain them as an occupying force until a new political leadership emerged in the South. And where the one would leave the black subservient, the other would elevate him to new status. Said the Old Commoner:

> We have turned, or are about to turn, loose four million slaves without a hut to shelter them or a cent in their pockets. The infernal laws of slavery have prevented them from acquiring an education, understanding the common laws of contract, or of managing the ordinary business of life. If we do not furnish them with homesteads, and hedge them around with protective laws; if we leave them to the legislation of their late masters, we had better leave them in bondage.

Stevens had already designed a plan for changing all this. Of the 6 million whites in the South, he pointed out, 70,000 families owned more than 200 acres of land each. Adding their land to that owned by the states themselves, the total was 394 million of the 465 million acres in the South. In confiscating this property the federal government would leave unhurt more than nine-tenths of the southern whites. But from the expropriated land, Stevens would give the million black families forty acres each, plus $50 in cash—for a mule or whatever. The rest would be sold to provide pensions for Union soldiers, to reimburse northern loyalists for lost property, and mostly—$3 billion—to pay off the national debt.

No sooner had Congress reconvened in December 1865 than

Freed blacks coming into Union lines in North Carolina. (Library of Congress)

Stevens and the radical Republicans sought to undo the President's "restorationist" mischief. The elected Confederate leaders were denied their seats in Congress. Two months later the Old Commoner had a resolution passed establishing a joint committee of the House and Senate to oversee reconstruction. He was its chairman. The resolution took from the President the right to determine when a secessionist state should be readmitted, and conferred it on Congress alone.

In short order, usually over presidential vetoes, the jubilant radicals put on the books the Civil Rights Act assuring legal equality to former slaves; the Freedmen's Bureau Act, which provided aid for ex-slaves for another two years; and the Fourteenth Amendment, which conferred full citizenship on blacks and guaranteed them "due process of law."

Discarding Johnson's civilian governments, Congress divided the ten states (Tennessee was not included) into five military districts, each ruled by a brigadier general. Twenty thousand soldiers, reinforced by militias formed from blacks, occupied the "conquered provinces" much as American troops did Germany and Japan after World War II. The Stevens-controlled Congress also passed a Tenure of Office Act in March 1867, prohibiting the President from removing cabinet members without consent of the legislature. This was aimed at preventing Johnson from replacing the Secretary of War, Edwin M. Stanton, who was in charge of reconstruction.

In carrying out the militant policy, there was doubtless much corruption by "carpetbaggers" (white radicals from the North) and "scalawags" (white radicals from the South). But there was also solid progress for the blacks. The Black Codes were rescinded. Six governors and thousands of lesser officials were removed from office. Military tribunals replaced civilian courts where necessary to guarantee the black against violence.

Tens of thousands of white Confederates were disfranchised; many others refused to vote though given the chance. When registration began in 1867, blacks on the new voting lists outnumbered whites 700,000 to 650,000. The former slaves did not gain political power, but episodically from 1868 to 1873 they did hold majorities in the lower houses of three states, and from 1869 to 1877 they were able to elect fourteen federal congressmen and two United States senators.

Conventions in the ten states drew up new constitutions considerably more democratic than those they replaced. At the same time, the Bureau of Freedmen, Refugees, and Abandoned Lands built forty hospitals, gave out 21 million packets of food (one-fourth of it to poor whites), opened 4,329 schools for 247,333 black pupils, and wrote tens of thousands of labor contracts spelling out employer obligations to black employees.

The militant mood was also sustained by the Union Leagues and Negro militia. The leagues were composed of ex-soldiers, workers of the Freedmen's Bureau, poor whites, and ex-slaves. There were 800 leagues in Virginia alone, preaching equality and agitating for confiscation of rebel property and division of the land among black folk.

Parallel to the leagues were the Negro militia, formed after 1867 under such names as the Whangs and the Wide-Awakers. They were usually volunteer groups made up of a nucleus of black soldiers who had served with the Union army, as well as civilian freedmen. Their role was to protect blacks from violence.

In the tense atmosphere of reconstruction, the Afro-Americans had much to defend themselves from. During the 1866 riots in Memphis, Charleston, and New Orleans, for instance, literally hundreds of blacks were shot down by police and white mobs. Fourteen regiments of "nigger K.K.K.'s"—as southern newsmen called the militias—were organized under the reconstruction government in South Carolina alone, each with 1,000 men. There were others, of course, elsewhere.

But despite the freedmen's bureau, the militia, the leagues, and a sympathetic Congress, the black man never received his forty acres and a mule. Stevens introduced a bill for land confiscation in 1867, based on his proposals of two years before. But he could not muster the necessary support for so drastic a measure.

At a time when millions of acres of land were being given away in the West—under the Homestead Act—and millions more to the railroads, Congress refused to vote forty acres for each black family. To cede virgin land that belonged to no one (except the Indian perhaps) was one thing. But to make grants from the property of yesterday's enemy was something else. Not even Stevens' fellow radicals were ready to tamper with so hallowed an institution as private property.

The only way for the ex-slave to get land, therefore, was through purchase—if he had any money—or through lease from the freedmen's bureau. Under the bill creating the bureau, the War Department was authorized to lease plots of forty acres or less at a rental of 6 percent of the land's value. Since it acquired only 800,000 acres of "abandoned lands," it could at best accommodate 20,000 blacks—a small number considering the million families crying for farms.

By this time the southern aristocrats, or "Bourbons," as they were called, were challenging reconstruction through all sorts of terrorist groups—the Ku Klux Klan, the Knights of the White Camellia, the Constitutional Union Guards, the Pale Faces. The number of murders committed by such groups ran into the thousands; in 1871, for instance, 300 blacks were killed near New Orleans alone, and 163 in one Florida county.

The Grant Administration took countermeasures. It disbanded the Ku Klux Klan in 1869 and the Knights of the White Camellia the following year. It passed Enforcement Acts in 1870 and 1871. But the number of southern whites convicted for violence was relatively small, and the intimidation continued. From 1870 to 1876 only 1,208 were adjudged guilty, mostly in Mississippi and South Carolina, where the radicals still held sway. More than twice that many went free.

Up north, too, radical passions were cooling. The rampaging financiers, hailed in history as the "Robber Barons," were not particularly interested in the black man's welfare. In fact they were a little afraid he might form an alliance with poor white laborers above the Mason-Dixon line. These sentiments steadily penetrated Republican ranks. In 1870-71 the radicals registered their last victories, with the Enforcement Acts and the Fifteenth Amendment to the Constitution guaranteeing the right to vote.

The white supremacists in the South regained in peace what they had lost in war. They had been weakened, of course, but they were on the mend. In 1869 Tennessee fell back into Bourbon hands. By 1876 all but three of the eleven Confederate states were sovereign—and racist.

That was the year when the presidential election was thrown into Congress. In the campaign between Republican Rutherford B. Hayes and Democrat Samuel Tilden, the twenty electoral votes of Oregon, South Carolina, Florida, and Louisiana were disputed. Tilden needed only one of these votes to win; Hayes needed all twenty. To get them, the Republican candidate promised the southern states to withdraw all federal troops from their territory and leave their destiny in the hands of the old aristocracy. From then on, for many decades to come, the blacks lost their right to vote, and whatever dream they cherished of economic security.

Physical liberation and liberation from poverty, it became apparent in the next quarter of a century, were not the same thing. In point of fact the black man was in a new form of bondage differing only slightly from the past—and in some ways worse. Frederick Douglass reported after a tour of the South in 1888 that former slaves were still in virtual servitude to their former masters. They were held that way by a device called the "trucking system": instead of paying wages in dollars, the former masters paid in scrip redeemable only at a single store, often owned by the employer himself. In other words, the black man or woman received no cash, only little pieces of paper (scrip) giving him or her the right to buy necessities at that one store. Not only were the former slaves overcharged, but since they had no actual money they could hardly take time off to find work elsewhere. "A blind man," wrote Douglass, "can see that by this arrangement the laborer is bound hand and foot, and he is completely in the power of his employer."

With the aid of the courts and as a result of terror against the blacks that went unpunished, the South was recast in its old image. Judge J. J. Chrisman, a man of the old school, admitted in 1890 that there had not been a fair election in Mississippi since 1875: "In plain words, we have been stuffing ballot-boxes, committing perjury and here and there in the State carrying the elections by fraud and violence."

Not atypical was the murder of thirty Louisiana blacks in the 1878 elections. From 1889 to 1918, 2,522 Afro-Americans were lynched in the South. A new term became familiar—"Jim Crow." How the term originated is not certain, but its meaning was clear.

Blacks were Jim Crowed—segregated—on passenger trains, in waiting rooms, restaurants, hospitals, everywhere. Black nurses were forbidden to treat white patients, and white nurses to treat black patients.

In the well-known *Plessy* v. *Ferguson* decision of 1896 the Supreme Court upheld the doctrine of "separate but equal" schools. The states were not required to integrate schools or other facilities so long as the facilities were "equal." In practice that meant inferior.

In a number of respects conditions became worse than in the heyday of slavery. Black prisoners, instead of being sent to jail, were leased out to favored politicians, then subleased to farms and factories as unpaid labor. Whipping and other forms of punishment cut the life span of such prisoners so that 32 percent died in 1887 in Arkansas, 16 percent in Mississippi. It was not until 1918 that this convict-lease system was abrogated.

A half century after the Civil War half the blacks of the nation were still illiterate. Some three-quarters of Afro-American farmers were sharecroppers or tenants, paying half of more of their crop to a white landlord in return for using his land, mule, and plow. Only the least desirable jobs went to the descendants of slaves, as attested to by the fact that one-third of employed blacks were domestic servants.

A dark gloom settled over black America.

10

Farming the Farmers

In 1862, the year Lincoln signed the Emancipation Proclamation, he also signed the Homestead Act and a bill to complete the transcontinental railroad. These three measures should have laid the basis for ending poverty in America. The proclamation freed 4 million blacks. The Homestead Act gave Americans a chance to get land, just for the asking. The railroad made transportation and shipping incredibly easy compared with the past.

Taken together, the three measures constituted an impressive antipoverty program. They were enormously popular. Yet, as already noted, the Emancipation Proclamation "freed the slave but ignored the Negro." The homestead law fell far short of the dreams of George Henry Evans. And the much celebrated "iron horse"—the railroad—became the most hated institution of the times.

Within a decade or two there was massive poverty in the Great West. During the 1880's and 1890's a stream of covered wagons headed back east. Some carried placards that read, "In God we trusted, in Kansas we busted"; or, "Going back to the wife's folks." The only crop raised in eastern Colorado for many years, it was said, was "bankrupts." A verse, published by the Farmers Alliance in 1889, stated:

> There are ninety and nine who live and die
> In want, and hunger, and cold.
> That one may live in luxury
> And be wrapped in silken fold.
> The ninety and nine in hovels bare,
> The one in a palace with riches rare.

By and large the millions who took Horace Greeley's advice to "go West" did not get their land free but bought it from a railroad or a speculator. Between them, the railroads and the speculators gained title to a half billion of the billion acres in the public domain.

The speculators got it in a dozen different ways. For instance, under the Morrill Act, Congress granted the states 140 million acres as endowments for agricultural colleges. That land could have been sold in small tracts to actual settlers, but almost invariably the states put the land on the market in large parcels, which were then gobbled up by landjobbers. Another method was for speculators to bribe public officials to permit registry of homesteads in the name of dummy holders.

The railroads, however, were far and away the greatest single beneficiary of government generosity. From 1850 to 1871 alone the rail carriers were given 137 million acres—an area as large as France, or five times the size of New York State. The one grant to the Northern Pacific Railway, in 1864, was equal in area to the six New England States.

Thus the best parts of the public domain—because they were near the railroad—were not free. Emigrants to the West preferred to buy a farm close to transportation, rather than stake a claim far away.

The railroads lured large numbers of people to their territory with deceptive advertising. The Atchison, Topeka, & Santa Fe claimed that a man could double his money in a single year if he purchased its land. The Illinois Central boasted that its million acres were "not surpassed by any in the world." The Burlington & Missouri told of people who had left New York with next to nothing now "living almost in affluence on their prairie farms." Settlers who were worried about the dry climate in

Completion of the Union Pacific Railroad: the ceremony at Promontory Point, Utah, May 10, 1869. (Library of Congress)

A railroad poster. (Library of Congress)

The waiting room of the Union Pacific Railroad depot, Omaha.
(Library of Congress)

Nebraska were told false tales about the great amount of rainfall.

Prices for the land varied, but were usually modest. Burlington sold its holdings in Nebraska for about $5 an acre; Illinois Central's "superior" lands went for $8 to $12 an acre. Interest rates were also fairly low. The railroads wanted the West settled, so as to increase their business, and they made it fairly simple. With such enticements, therefore, the trans-Mississippi population swelled rapidly. The four grain-raising territories—Minnesota, Dakota, Nebraska, and Kansas—grew from 300,000 to nearly a million by 1870, and 2½ million by 1880.

Hopeful people came, historian Allan Nevins tells us, "in almost penniless estate, with few tools, little household furniture and no conveniences. Many lived for years in dugouts, an excavation perhaps a dozen feet wide in the side of a hill. . . ." They cleared the land, planted it, and harvested the crop—working sunup to sundown much of the year.

But how were they to know about such things as overproduction—that the more they grew, the more they were lowering prices?

There were good years and bad years, but Department of Agriculture statistics show that cotton fell relentlessly, from 15.1 cents per pound in 1870–73 to 5.8 cents in 1894–97. Corn was 75.3 cents in 1869 and 28.3 cents in 1889; oats were 43.3 cents in 1870 and 22.9 cents in 1889; and wheat fluctuated from $1.04 to 69.8 cents between the years 1870 and 1889. The plight of the western farmer is conveyed in a single dry statistic: in 1867, a crop of 1.3 billion bushels of cereals (corn, wheat, rye, oats, barley, and buckwheat) was raised on 66 million acres. It brought farmers a return of $1.3 billion. In 1887, the crop was twice as large (2.7 billion bushels), grown on 142 million acres, but it brought in less money—$1.2 billion.

No matter which way the pendulum swung, the American farmer seemed to be at the wrong end. There was a boom during and immediately after the Civil War, and high prices drew migrants to the West like a magnet. But by 1870 the supply of commodities had overtaken demand, prices fell, and the farmer had less money to repay his debts. The depression from 1873 to 1879 caught him square in the midriff.

By the time the economy had returned to normal, the overpopulated West faced a new antagonist: competition from Australia, Argentina, Russia, and Canada. Bumper domestic wheat crops in 1882 and 1884 were canceled out by a big drop in exports, causing a corresponding downturn in prices.

After 1887, drought beset Nebraska, Kansas, and South Dakota. Where rainfall had averaged 21.63 inches in previous years, it sometimes fell to as little as 2 or 3 inches in the next decade. Nebraska produced 129 million bushels of corn in 1885 but 13 million in 1894.

Surveying the wreckage of early hopes, Mary Elizabeth Lease, the populist leader from Wichita, Kansas, advised farmers "to raise less corn and more hell."

The problems of overpopulation and overproduction were not the only ones. The main sources of discontent were due to the railroads and the mortgage holders. "There are three great crops in Nebraska," a farmer wrote in 1890. "One is a crop of corn, one a crop of freight rates, and one a crop of interest. One is produced by farmers who by sweat and toil farm the land. The other two are produced by men who sit in their offices and behind their bank counters and farm the farmers."

The farmers hailed the railroad originally as friend and ally. Innumerable tillers of the soil invested in railroad stocks, often mortgaging their farms to do so, and local communities offered big bounties to have the rail lines run through their territories.

It soon became apparent, however, that far too many railroad promoters were bribing and manipulating their way to riches on a scale unmatched before. Typically, in Wisconsin the La Crosse & Milwaukee Railroad passed around a million dollars in bonds and cash to thirteen senators, thirty assemblymen, the governor (he got $50,000), and various newsmen to assure a $17 million land grant.

The Crédit Mobilier scandal, exposed in 1872, was an extreme example of corruption, but differed only in details from similar practices elsewhere. A month and a half after Lincoln signed the Homestead Act, Congress took steps to complete a transcontinental railroad system. The section from Omaha to California was assigned to the specially organized Union Pacific Railroad; Congressman Oakes Ames of Massachusetts was one of the stockholders and the key figure in the scandal.

Ames spread around $436,000 in bribes to such legislators as Senator James G. Blaine, future President James A. Garfield, and others. Congress reacted generously. It gave Union Pacific 200 feet right-of-way for hundreds of miles; the right to use whatever wood, stone, and other materials it found nearby; gifts of alternate sections of land running twenty miles on either side of the tracks; and credits of $16,000 to $48,000 for each mile of track laid.

The men associated with Ames were not satisfied with this. They formed a company with the French name Crédit Mobilier to build the railroad. It cost Crédit Mobilier $50 million to construct the line. In turn it charged Union Pacific $94 million, netting a profit for Ames and his friends of $44 million. Ames was not wrong when he said he had hit "a diamond mine."

Another means of swindling the public was to "water" the stock. The Erie Railroad, for instance, had a value of approximately $17 million in assets, but it sold $78 million in stock to the public. The extra millions went to the promoters. They were able to get away with such practices through bribes and by controlling local and state governments. Historians are agreed that in the early years every western state was at one time or another in the vest pocket of the carriers. The Union Pacific and Burlington railroads jointly controlled Nebraska; the Santa Fe ran Kansas.

Someone, of course, had to pay for the corruption and the excessive profits. The powerless farmer was the obvious choice. Most of the railroads held monopolies in their territories, and where they did not, made pooling arrangements with competitors to maintain high freight charges. The farmer was squeezed by these discriminatory rates.

To ship a bushel of corn to market from Kansas, Nebraska, or Iowa cost at least the equivalent of another bushel, sometimes much more. In 1869, when corn was sold for 70 cents in the East, shipping charges from the Mississippi Valley were 52½ cents—leaving the farmer only 17½ cents for himself.

There were other forms of mischief. Short hauls, for instance, were sometimes more expensive than longer ones; wheat could be transported from Minneapolis to Chicago for half as much as from Fargo to Duluth, though the distance was twice as far. Large shippers, in league with the carriers, received rebates, while small farmers paid the normal freight rates. Something was obviously wrong. At a time when corn brought 80 cents or a dollar a bushel in eastern markets, Iowa farmers were burning it, instead of coal, because they were being offered only 15 cents.

Not too far behind the railroads as an object of the farmers' wrath were the mortgage holders and merchants. The farmer needed credit—to pay off last year's debts, buy new equipment, or build a barn. Fortunately there was enough loose money back east to fill his needs. Massachusetts mortgagers, it is estimated, loaned western tillers $8 million to $12 million annually. New Hampshire held $25 million in trans-Mississippi land mortgages as of 1899. The amount of credit from lenders in states like New York was very much larger.

The trouble with this system was that rural America was living in cycles of boom and bust. When the farm economy was lively and land values rising, investors gladly provided mortgage money. But when times were bad, the money well dried up and the farmer was left near bankruptcy. The worst of these boom-bust cycles came to a head in the prairie states in 1887.

The year began with wild speculation. A farm purchased in Abilene, Kansas, for $6.25 an acre in 1867 was peddled twenty years later for $270 an acre. Land three miles from the center of Kansas City was sold for $5,000 an acre; and seven miles out, for $1,500. A Wichita clerk bought a lot for $200 one day and sold it for $2,000 two months later. The prospect of quick profits brought 35,000 people to Wichita from January to May 1887, and resulted in real estate sales of $35 million.

But within a few weeks things turned sour, when it became apparent that the crop of 1887 would be a disaster. With farmers unable to meet their loans, land values dropped as quickly as they had risen. Farmers sold their cattle for anything they could get, and tried to negotiate chattel mortgages on machinery, horses, or any other property—at interest rates of 20 to 36 percent a year.

It did no good, however. In Kansas, the state with the biggest boom and loudest bust, 11,122 foreclosures took place from 1889 to 1893. By 1895 there were fifteen counties where between 76 and 90 percent of the land had fallen into the hands of loan companies. This was the period when 180,000 inhabitants deserted the state, "going back to the wife's folks." Twenty towns were totally depopulated.

A letter to the Farmers' Alliance of Lincoln, Nebraska, dated January 10, 1891, tells a not too uncommon story:

> The hot winds burned up the entire crop, leaving thousands of families wholly destitute, many of whom might have been able to run through this crisis had it not been for the galling yoke put on them by the money loaners and sharks—not by charging seven percent per annum, which is the lawful rate of interest, or even ten percent, but the unlawful and inhuman country-destroying-rate of three percent a month, some going still further and charging fifty percent per annum.

The credit system in the southern states was just as bad—or worse. The largest number of farmers were sharecroppers. They leased a "one-horse" or "two-horse" farm (fifteen to forty acres) and received from their landlord seed, tools, and a horse or mule, to operate it. For this the sharecropper paid the landlord one-half of the cotton or corn he produced. Or, if he used his own animals and tools, he paid one-fourth to one-third.

The sharecropper had no property to put up as security for loans. His only credit therefore came from the merchant. The merchant advanced him what he needed from the store—flour, bacon, and so forth. At harvest time the sharecropper brought his crop to the merchant to be sold. Out of this money the account was settled.

The trouble with this system was that the sharecropper couldn't buy anywhere else, and he was therefore forced to pay $5 a barrel for flour that sold elsewhere for $4; or 12½ cents a pound for bacon that could be bought in other stores for 10 cents. Since the average period of the "loan" was six months, the overcharge actually amounted to interest of 40 to 100 percent a year.

The result of this form of credit was that the sharecropper was always in hock to the merchant—and the merchant ran his life. He had to consult the merchant on what crops to grow, and agree to do all his buying and selling through that one store.

The 'cropper was never out of debt, and lived from year to year only a step removed from utter destitution.

The striking feature of poverty in the South and West in the last third of the nineteenth century was that it grew side by side with great prosperity and major technological advances. The development of barbed wire for fencing material made it possible for farmers to populate the prairies (otherwise it might have fallen entirely to the cowboys and the roaming herds). The windmill partially solved the problem of water. The reaper, the twine binder, the combine, the bundle carrier, the straddle row cultivator, the seeder, and many other machines made it possible to increase grain production from 5.6 bushels for every person in the nation in 1860 to 9.2 bushels in 1880.

The railroads, which increased their trackage from 35,000 miles before the Civil War to 200,000 by the end of the century, simplified travel and marketing. The United States economy, despite

Harvest hands on their way to the wheat fields of the Northwest. (Library of Congress)

depressions, was in an unparalleled upswing. Population doubled from 1860 to 1890; wealth quadrupled; industrial production rose five times; and deposits in savings banks rose ten times.

Yet the farmer—mostly native-born, incidentally, not immigrant—failed to reap the harvest.

"I take my pen in hand," a Kansas woman wrote Governor Lorenzo D. Lewelling of Kansas in 1894, "to let you know that we are starving to death. . . . I haven't had nothing to eat today and it is three o'clock!"

Only one good thing came out of the poverty on the farms in this period: it resulted in a revulsion against the idea of laissez-faire—that the government must leave businessmen and railroads alone to do as they pleased. It led to the formation of farmer movements and progressive city movements which decades later changed the character of American society. In the process of organizing themselves, the rural poor of the 1880's and 1890's laid the cornerstone for populism, as well as the "Square Deal," "New Freedom," "New Deal," "New Frontier," that were to follow.

11

Hayseed Socialism

In the three decades after the Civil War, discontented farmers formed a variety of movements to defend themselves. The Grange, the Greenback Party, the Alliance, the People's Party (Populists), fought for regulation of the railroads, currency reform, and many other changes. Essentially, what they tried to do was to put the government on the side of the poor rather than the rich.

It was well and good, said the Populist leaders, to talk about laissez-faire—leave alone. But in fact the government did not leave alone the corporations and special interests. It helped them in a hundred ways—through class legislation and favoritism. That was not what the United States Constitution meant, said the farm leaders, when it spoke about promoting the general welfare.

They claimed that the first duty of government is to the weak —the farmers, the poor, the workers. The federal government has the responsibility, they said, to regulate commerce, issue money, and take other actions so as to protect the natural rights of the many against the few. Though it may not sound so today, this was a dramatic idea at the time—a sharp departure from old concepts about individualism.

But hostile detractors called it "hayseed socialism."

The first of the hayseed organizations that swept the prairies went by the unwieldy name of the National Grange of the Patrons of Husbandry. It was more popularly known as "the Grange." By 1874 there were 20,000 local granges in thirty-two of the thirty-seven states, with 1½ million members. Considering that there were only 3 million farms then, this was no mean representation.

The Grange did many things. Lectures, songs, newspapers, and magazines provided both social relief and self-education for farmers. In times of stress—such as the flooding of the Mississippi in 1874—the Grange mobilized aid for rural victims.

Most of all, however, the Grange fought against monopolies. "Down with Monopoly" was among its most frequently heard slogans. The monopolies were challenged in three ways: through the formation of Grange businesses and cooperatives, through politics, and through the sponsorship of laws to regulate railroads (commonly known as the "Granger Laws").

Beginning with 1869, the Mississippi Valley "Granger states"

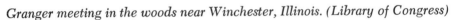

Granger meeting in the woods near Winchester, Illinois. (Library of Congress)

passed bills setting "just, reasonable, and uniform" freight rates. Regulation of any business was then considered a novelty. Under the theory of laissez-faire, the government was supposed to leave business alone. Pursuing the argument, the rail carriers cried that regulation violated the Fourteenth Amendment: it deprived them of property without due process of law. Railroad lawyers said that the carriers were private companies, who should not be subject to regulation any more than a merchant who sold candles or calico.

The issue went to the courts, which sometimes upheld the legislation, at other times declared it unconstitutional. It was many years before the regulation of railroads became an accepted fact of life as it is today.

Though the Grange did not engage directly in politics, it encouraged third-party movements in eleven states. These third parties went under such names as the "Anti-Monopoly," "Reform," or "Independent" Party, and from time to time elected Congressmen and a few senators to the national legislature, as well as many local officials. Kansas in particular was heavily disposed toward Grange politics.

The Grange also fostered a wide variety of cooperatives in order to provide farmers with cheaper goods. By eliminating the middleman, Illinois granges were able to sell reapers for $175 while private retailers were charging $275. Small threshers that ordinarily sold for $300 could be bought from the Grange for $200; $150 wagons for $90; sewing machines for little more than half the price charged by private firms.

So extensive were the Grange's businesses—both cooperatives and those directly operated by the Grange—that the *Chicago Tribune* in 1874 carried three columns of advertisements listing the Grange's services. Included were insurance, elevators for grain, gristmills, pork-packing facilities, and harvesters. At its peak the Iowa grange operated three plow factories at Des Moines and owned thirty grain elevators.

The Grange began to lose ground in 1875, in the midst of the long depression that had begun in 1873. Its program no longer seemed militant enough to the average farmer.

The next phase of agrarian revolt, overlapping the Grange period to an extent, was an organized campaign for inflation—the greenback movement.

During the Civil War the federal government issued $450 million in paper dollars, called "greenbacks." Because the greenbacks had no gold or silver behind them, they depreciated in value. Each dollar, in other words, bought less and less goods. Or, put another way, prices went up.

Most farmers were pleased with this result. Not only did the price of their grain or cattle rise, but they were able to pay off old loans with cheap money. Suppose a farmer had borrowed $100 when wheat was $1 a bushel, and paid it off when wheat had gone to $2 a bushel. His loan originally was the equivalent of 100 bushels; now he paid back the equivalent of only 50 bushels.

The bankers and other creditors, of course, were opposed to depreciated money. When President Grant withdrew most of the greenbacks from circulation, the bankers applauded; the farmers were blue with anger. When Grant also paid Wall Street bondholders gold for their bonds—rather than greenbacks—the farmers became even more angry. The cry went up for "the same currency for the bondholder and the ploughholder."

The greenback movement began with the formation of the National Labor Reform Party in 1871–72. That party was short-lived and ill-fated. In March 1875 the Independent Party was launched; it became generally known as the "Greenback Party." In addition to cheap money, the Greenbackers called for a shorter workday for laborers, a land policy guaranteeing land only to settlers, discontinuance of contract prison labor, and other reforms. But cheap money was their religion.

The Greenbackers polled a million votes for Congress in the 1878 elections—11 percent of the total. Their candidate for President in 1880, General James B. Weaver, didn't do as well—he received only 3 percent of the vote.

Nonetheless the greenback movement attracted many prominent people. Among them was Adlai E. Stevenson, who later became Vice-President under Grover Cleveland. Stevenson was the

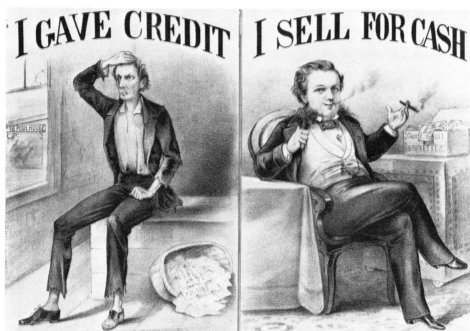

'TWAS HIM.

THE WAY TO GROW POOR.

Cartoons depict the economic and political scene of the 1870's. (Library of Congress)

THE WAY TO GROW RICH.

grandfather of the Democratic presidential nominee of 1952 and 1956, and the great-grandfather of the present Senator from Illinois. Others included the famous suffragette leader Susan B. Anthony; General B. F. Butler; the millionaire Peter Cooper; Ignatius Donnelly, a colorful lawyer and congressman from Minnesota; and the equally colorful General Weaver, also a congressman and an authentic Civil War hero.

The high point of the agrarian revolt was reached in the 1890's, when the People's Party was formed, but it was preceded by all kinds of populist organizations, the most prominent of which were the alliances.

The Southern Alliance was organized by a remarkable young man named C. W. Macune. The Northern Alliance was led by Milton George, an Illinois farmer turned newspaper editor. (They refused to merge only because the southerners wouldn't include blacks in their ranks.) By 1892 there were 2 million members in the alliances.

The alliances bore striking resemblance to the Grange—with the one difference that they were more openly political. They avidly recruited women, arranged the usual picnics and social affairs, sent lecturers to the hustings to advise on scientific farming and crop rotation, opened libraries to encourage "a general system of home culture," published 800 newspapers (150 in Kansas alone), formed cooperatives, and engaged in a dozen kinds of business enterprise, including grain elevators, insurance companies, and creameries. Beyond this, the alliances agitated against the railroads—which still fought regulation tooth and nail—and, most important, in favor of cheap money. Money reform by now no longer centered on the greenback but on the coinage of silver.

Back in 1837 Congress had agreed to mint silver at a value of sixteen to one in relation to gold—371.25 grains of pure silver to a dollar, as against 23.22 grains of pure gold. But as the amount of silver on the market expanded, its price dropped. In 1876 a silver dollar was worth only 90 cents compared with a gold dollar, 72 cents in 1889, and 60 cents in 1893. The farmer, thinking of sal-

Wall Street during the Panic of 1884. (Library of Congress)

vation in terms of inflation, was pleased with the silver money. He demanded that the government coin all the silver it could lay its hands on. Depreciating the value of money would increase the price a farmer received for his commodities.

To win monetary reform (as well as railroad regulation, federal ownership of the telegraph, abolition of national banks, the breakup of monopolies), the alliances turned to politics. In the South especially, they had remarkable success working inside the Democratic Party. By 1890 alliance men and women dominated the Democratic Party conventions in Florida, Georgia, and the two Carolinas, and controlled five southern legislatures. They also elected three governors, one United States senator, and forty-four Congressmen.

In the Northwest the Alliance functioned outside the two-party system. It put forth tickets under such names as "Independent Party," "People's Party," "Industrial Party." It was not as influential as its southern counterpart, but even so it recorded important victories. The People's Independent Party of Nebraska captured both legislative houses. Minnesota elected a populist congressman. Kansas and South Dakota chose favorable United States senators. The most noteworthy success was in Kansas, where populism captured the lower house and elected five members to Congress.

Hayseed socialism was now ripe for national harvest. It came to a climax in Omaha on July 4, 1892, where a convention was held to launch a People's Party.

The largest contingent at this convention came, of course, from the alliances. But there were also representatives from the Knights of Labor, suffragettes, single-taxers, and many others. It was a lively convention, given to singing at the drop of a hat. According to a reporter, when Ignatius Donnelly finished reading the platform preamble, "there was enacted the mightiest scene ever witnessed by the human race. Fifteen thousand people yelled, shrieked, threw papers, hats, fans, and parasols, gathered up banners, mounted shoulders." The ovation lasted forty minutes.

The preamble went as follows:

> We meet in the midst of a nation brought to the verge of moral, political and material ruin. Corruption dominates the ballot-box, the legislatures, the Congress, and touches even the ermine of the bench. . . . The fruits of the toil of millions are boldly stolen to build up colossal fortunes for a few . . . the possessors of these, in turn, despise the republic and endanger liberty. From the same prolific womb of governmental injustice we breed the two great classes—tramps and millionaires. . . .

The key points in the platform called for "free and unlimited coinage of silver and gold at the present legal ratio of sixteen to one," and an interesting system of loans to farmers.

Under the "subtreasury plan" devised by C. W. Macune, the government would put money in circulation through subtreasury offices. Here a farmer could bring his crop and receive a cash loan on it—up to 80 percent of the value of his corn, cotton, wheat—at 1 percent a year interest. If he wished, he could redeem his produce within a year. Or he could sell his deposit certificate. This plan, said Macune, was no different from the system already being used to issue money. Under the prevailing system bankers deposited bonds with the United States Treasurer and were given the right to issue money up to 90 percent of the value of the bonds. Macune wanted that right to work in favor of farmers as well.

The program of the Omaha assemblage also called for the graduated income tax; postal savings banks; government ownership and operation of the railroads, telephones, and telegraph; a shorter workweek; and the reclamation of land held by railroads and corporations "in excess of their actual needs." It was a program designed to redistribute income, wealth, and power in favor of the lower classes. Not unexpectedly it was greeted with a "cyclonic ovation." The man selected to present it for the consideration of the American voters was General Weaver of Greenbacker fame.

Weaver polled only 1,041,028 votes for President in 1892—a disappointing 9 percent of the total. Why he did so poorly was a subject of much debate, since the alliance membership alone should have guaranteed 2 or 3 million votes. Nonetheless, even this result had some effect. The older parties began to cater to populist sentiment. Both the Democrats and Republicans included a silver plank in their platforms that year. In the congressional elections of 1894, the Populists received nearly 1½ million votes.

By 1896 the populist mood was for an all-or-nothing gamble. The People's Party joined with the Democrats, who agreed with them on the silver issue, in an effort to seize the White House. They nominated Democrat William Jennings Bryan, a thirty-six-year old spellbinder from Nebraska, to run as joint candidate of both parties.

Populism had now reached its apogee. Bryan failed by only 600,000 votes in his effort to defeat Republican William McKinley. He ran again in 1900, with Adlai E. Stevenson for Vice-President, and received approximately the same number of tallies.

From that point on populism disintegrated. Its adherents had won twenty-seven seats in Congress in 1896, but only ten in 1898, and none in 1902. The People's Party candidate for President in 1904, Tom Watson, secured a mere 117,183 votes. One by one, the leaders of the movement returned to the fold of the old parties.

What really cut the ground from under populism was farm prosperity. From 1899 to 1909 crops increased in value from $3 billion to $5½ billion; the worth of farm property rose from approximately $20 billion to $40 billion.

But populism had left its mark. Though it disappeared, its agitation resulted in many reforms. Surveying the results years later, in 1914, Mary Elizabeth Lease said:

> I have seen, with gratification, that my work in the good old Populist days was not in vain. . . . Note the list of reforms which we advocated which are coming into reality. Di-

rect election of senators is assured. Public utilities are gradually removed from the hands of the few and placed under the control of the people who use them. Woman suffrage is now almost a national issue. . . . The seed we sowed in Kansas did not fall on barren ground.

Ms. Lease overstated the case, but populism could boast important victories. Woman suffrage did win out. So did the Australian (secret) ballot, and direct primaries in many states. Populism's silver plank prodded government leaders to reform the money system by passing the Federal Reserve Act. The government did not seize the railroads, but the Interstate Commerce Commission was finally given the power to set rates and abolish discriminatory practices.

The major significance of populism as a program against poverty, however, was not in what it achieved directly, but in starting the national dialogue over the role of government. For the next two-thirds of a century this was perhaps the most important item of political discussion. Populism was the opening act of a long drama.

12

The Other Half

Books on the United States emphasize what is called "upward mobility." They tell us how the indentured servant became a landowner, the journeyman a capitalist. The newsboy saved his dimes and became an oil magnate; the grocery clerk married the boss's daughter and became a merchant. If today's poor man did not make it, his son or grandson would. There were shining examples of men like Andrew Carnegie who catapulted from rags to riches in a few decades.

All this is true—and untrue. In the long history of the United States, many millions of families did move upward, and still do. But parallel to this process, many millions more stayed poor or became poor.

The first seventeen years of the twentieth century, up to World War I, give an excellent illustration of how upward mobility and frozen mobility went on at the same time. In these seventeen years wealth and poverty rose together, both reaching new peaks.

Millionaires grew like wild weeds. During the 1840's there were fewer than twenty, but there were 4,000 in 1902, according to *The World Almanac*. One percent of the people in the nation, it was estimated, owned half of its wealth.

Other people shared in the enlarging prosperity. The middle classes—doctors, lawyers, small businessmen—were certainly better off than they had been in the past. So too the 2 million skilled workers who belonged to the American Federation of Labor. Even the rural areas, which enjoyed good harvests after 1897, were showing signs of modest affluence. In the prairies one could see more well-kept buildings, newly painted barns, better roads, expensive machines.

But the center of American life was now the city, and here the cesspool of poverty became much larger and much worse. Just before the Civil War there had been only sixteen cities with a population of 50,000 or more; by 1910 there were more than a hundred. In these drab centers manufacturing volume was fifteen times greater and the number of wage earners almost five times larger. This was a grand technological success, but its grim side was appalling. Urban poverty had existed before, but never on the scale of the "Progressive Era"—the first decade and a half of the new century.

The city by now was a group of ghettos, famous at home and abroad for its sickening slums, disease, vice, crime, sweat shops, and privation. "The first city," wrote Josiah Strong in his book *The Twentieth Century City*, "was built by the first murderer, and crime and vice and wretchedness have festered in it ever since." In the city a man could work fifty-two weeks a year and still be poor and hungry.

The outstanding feature of the American city in the early twentieth century was its foreign character. Of New York's population in 1903, 37 percent were foreign-born; if you include those of foreign parentage, 80 percent. The same proportion prevailed in Chicago, and the ratio was even higher in Milwaukee. From 1900 to 1915, 13 million immigrants came to the United States; there were 1,285,000 in 1907 alone.

Previous immigrants had been natives of England, Scotland, Ireland, Germany, and Scandinavia. The new ones were mostly from southern and eastern Europe—Italians, Poles, Russians, eastern European Jews, and Czechs. The poet Edwin Markham described the immigrant of this period as a man who had:

Tenement sufferers enduring a sweltering night in New York. (Library of Congress)

> The emptiness of ages in his face,
> And on his back the burden of the world.

Many were illiterate, even in their own tongue. Half of those from the southern part of Italy and Sicily, for instance, could neither read nor write Italian, let alone English. They depended on immigrant societies and the political machines to get them jobs and cold-water flats, to teach them English and help them become citizens.

On arriving at Ellis Island, the foreigners were met by representatives of immigrant societies of their own ethnic group—Italian societies for the Italians, Jewish for the Jews, and so on. They were handed a little pamphlet welcoming them to "the best country in the world."

But native-born Americans—second-, third-, fourth-generation Americans—did not think of the immigrants so kindly. They called them "dagos," "mockies," "hunkies," and other derogatory terms. They accused them of working their heads off at low pay, and thereby depressing wages for everyone else.

The immigrant of this period, then, began his life in America with many strikes against him. The environment was more hostile than he expected. And though he held the hope that his children would eventually melt into the melting pot, he himself lived meanwhile in stultifying want.

One of the plagues confronted by the immigrant was the "padrone" system. The padrone was an agent who usually had an ally in Europe recruiting potential workers for the United States. When these newcomers arrived in New York or Boston or wherever, the padrone found living quarters for them as well as a job—all, of course, at a handsome commission.

The system operated much like a cattle market. A road contractor or a railroad builder in need of unskilled labor placed an order with a padrone for, say, "five hundred dagos." The padrone supplied them for so much per "dago." No matter how bad the job was or how distant from home, the illiterate foreigner was usually afraid to reject it. He didn't know his way around or how to find work elsewhere.

As often as not, the jobs supplied by the padrones were akin to slave labor. Conditions were abysmal, but the foreign worker could not leave. A reporter for the *Charities Review* told of visiting some of the camps where immigrants supplied by padrones labored. The camps were in West Virginia, "cut off from the outside world by mountains." The contractor had paid the padrone $15 for each worker. To protect his investment, he placed armed guards around the camps to stop anyone from fleeing. One man who ran away was caught and "driven back at a run under the muzzle of a rifle, and made to lift alone so heavy a stone that he suffered a severe rupture."

Tens of thousands of immigrants were victimized by the padrones. The Italians suffered most, but the same was true of other ethnic groups. "Scarce a Greek comes here, man or boy," wrote Jacob A. Riis, "who is not under contract. A hundred dollars a year is the price. . . ."

It wasn't just the padrone system that made working conditions so bad. The city factory all too often was a hellhole—cold, dank, dirty, poorly ventilated, unsafe, a firetrap. Every now and then a tragedy would take place in one of these sweatshops that showed just how terrible conditions were.

On March 25, 1911, for instance, a fire broke out at the Triangle Shirtwaist Company in New York. In this poorly ventilated shop, with no outside fire escape and no fire sprinklers, 500 Jewish and Italian immigrant girls sat crowded back to back. The floors were littered with inflammable material; garbage was heaped everywhere. The toilets were outside the factory. On that day the company locked the steel door leading to the stairway, in order to prevent the girls from going to the toilets too often. At ten minutes to five, just before closing, fire broke out. There was no way to escape except by the freight elevators—or to jump from the windows. Of the trapped employees 145, mostly young girls, jumped to their deaths or were burned alive.

The heavy industries were no better. A Hungarian churchman described the steel mills of Pennsylvania this way:

Fourteen thousand tall chimneys are silhouetted against the sky along the valley that extends from McKeesport to Pittsburgh. . . . The realms of Vulcan could not be more somber or filthy than this valley of the Monongahela. . . . Scarce an hour passes without an accident, and no day without a fatal disaster. But what if *one* man is crippled, if *one* life be extinguished among so many!

There were ten men, said the count, ready to take the place of each one killed or injured.

That same year, according to Frederick L. Hoffman, statistician of the Prudential Life Insurance Company, there were 30,000 to 35,000 workers killed in job accidents. Occupational diseases such as silicosis, pulmonary and other respiratory ailments, arsenic and lead poisoning, caused many of these deaths. In addition 2 million workers were injured.

Another sign of the times was the employment of children. "Just think of it," said the superintendent of New York's public schools in 1903. "Think of today in these United States, children five and six years old, working from six in the morning until six in the evening, and at the hardest and most trying kind of labor. These children are being ruined by thousands of manufacturers."

In the New York canning factories boys and girls under fourteen worked from four in the morning until nine at night, snipping beans or husking corn. In Chicago's stockyards, according to a factory inspector, young boys under fourteen "act as butchers, sticking sheep, lambs, and swine. . . ." Some of these same boys took over dangerous machines when their fathers were hurt on the job—otherwise their parent would be fired. Professor William O. Krohn noted that "not a day passes but some child is made a helpless cripple" through an accident in the stamping works and canning factories.

At the turn of the century there were almost 300,000 children ten to fifteen years old employed in factories, mines, and mills. When some of them went on strike against textile mills in Philadelphia in 1903, they carried banners which said:

We Want to Go to School!
More Schools Less Hospitals!

Employment of children in violation of the law: tobacco strippers in a New York City tenement. (Library of Congress)

Prosperity! Where Is Our Share?

55 Hours or Nothing!

The slums where the immigrants lived were as bad as the sweatshops or overheated steel mills. The New York Tenement House Committee of 1900 made a report on slum conditions which gives some idea of the problem. Most of the tenements were six-story buildings on small twenty-five-foot lots. There were of course no elevators. Each floor had four flats that "[gave] its occupants less light and less ventilation, less fire protection and less comfortable surroundings than the average tenement of fifty years ago, which was lower in height, occupied less lot space, and sheltered fewer people."

In 1864 in New York, 486,000 persons lived in tenements. In 1900, 2,372,079 of the 3½ million New Yorkers were crowded into slums much worse. In a typical tenement there were fourteen rooms on each floor, but only four received light and air from the street or back yard. The ten rooms on the sides were fed air from a shaft "which is enclosed on all four sides, and is foul and semi-dark." In summer, "the small bedrooms are so hot and stifling that a large part of the tenement-house population sleeps on the roofs, the sidewalks, and the fire-escapes." On one block there were 605 apartments in thirty-nine tenements. There was not a single bathtub, and only forty apartments had hot water.

New York's Mulberry Street about 1888. (photograph by Jacob A. Riis, The Jacob A. Riis Collection, Museum of the City of New York)

A rear tenement bedroom around 1910. (photograph by Lewis Hine, International Museum of Photography at George Eastman House)

Many of these flats were not only homes but domestic factories where mother, children, and sometimes the father sewed garments, wrapped cigars, made artificial flowers, or did other home work. These conditions were duplicated in every big city.

A report of the Chicago City Homes Association shows that Chicago was just as bad as, or worse than, New York. The tenements there were not high; 90 percent were one or two stories.

But the overcrowding was indescribable. Three-quarters of the apartments studied had less than 400 square feet (20 by 20). In case after case there were seven or eight people living in 228 square feet or less—about as large as a medium-sized living room nowadays.

A young sociologist, Robert Hunter, visited the home of a man who did street paving and had come home early because of heat prostration. In the two-room apartment of a rear tenement (behind one fronting the street) lived seven people.

The day was in August [Hunter records], and the sun beat down upon one unintermittently and without mercy. . . . The air was steamy with a half-finished washing, and remnants of the last meal were still upon the table. A crying baby and the sick husband occupied the only bed.

As he watched the skillful mother keeping order in her household, writes Hunter, he

understood a little of what it meant to live in such contracted quarters. To cook and wash for seven, to nurse a crying baby broken out with heat, and to care for a delirious husband, to arrange a possible sleeping-place for seven, to do all these things in two rooms which open upon an alley, tremulous with heated odors and swarming with flies from the garbage and manure boxes, was something to tax the patience and strength of a Titan.

In the three districts he researched, "darkness, lack of air, uncleanliness, and poisonous gases" were a universal complaint. One out of every twelve families lived in dank, airless basements. The plumbing was abominable; of the rear 769 apartments, 667 had no sinks. Despite laws to the contrary, there were hundreds of privies that were nothing but holes in the ground without sewer connections—each one for eight or nine people.

Many of the water closets were in halls, basements, or under the sidewalks, releasing an insufferable stench that penetrated

Opposite: *A shoemaker.* Below: *Boy under the legal age at work in a sweatshop. (photographs by Jacob A. Riis, The Jacob A. Riis Collection, Museum of the City of New York)*

inside the apartments. In two Italian and Jewish neighborhoods, only 3 percent of the homes had bathtubs. Worst of all, there were "a surprising number of stables in the three districts." District one had 537 stables—almost one for every rear house—which housed 1,443 horses.

Here are some typical entries in the social workers' logbooks describing specific buildings on certain streets:

Polk Street—Cellar and first floor used for stables.

Twelfth Street—Stable complained of as the worst in America. Three cows kept in dilapidated house. Three cows and four horses kept in stable; shocking condition.

Taylor Street—Manure pile has been in yard over a year. Bitter complaints.

Liberty Street—Manure seven feet high in yard.

Blue Island Avenue—Manure-box bottom is broken out and manure falls to yard ten feet below. Yard wet and dirty.

Throop Street—Keep poultry in cellar, great odor.

What this state of affairs did to people can't be told in bare statistics. The inhabitants of slums suffered terribly from diseases such as tuberculosis. But there were other effects, including, as one New York agency reported, the following:

Keeping children up and out of doors until midnight in warm weather, because rooms are almost unendurable; making cleanliness of house and street difficult; filling the air with unwholesome emanations and foul odors of every kind; producing a state of nervous tension; interfering with the separateness of home life; leading to a promiscuous mixing of all ages and sexes in a single room, thus breaking down the barriers of modesty and conducing to the corruption of the young, and occasionally to revolting crimes.

It was no wonder, then, that "prostitution has spread greatly among the tenement houses." Daughters of "honest and reputable parents," said the New York Tenement House Committee, often envied the ladies of joy who plied their trade in the same buildings. "The fall of many girls . . . has, undoubtedly, been due to this contamination."

The slums enticed disenchanted youth into a life of crime. They drove some insane—half of the inmates of New York state's insane asylums were foreign-born slum dwellers. They drove others to the poorhouses—two-thirds of those in city poorhouses were aliens.

Statistics on economic growth or national income clearly did not tell the whole story. "To many thoughtful men" of the period, one historian notes, "it seemed that America in making her fortune was in peril of losing her soul."

It became apparent to many reformers during the early part of the twentieth century that it wasn't just the old, the sick, the blind, the helpless, who were poor. Millions who worked every day were also in want.

Among the writers who described such conditions were Jacob Riis, the author of *How the Other Half Lives;* Josiah Flynt; Owen Kildare; Charles B. Spahr; and A. M. Simons. In 1904 Robert Hunter published a book under the simple title *Poverty,* which changed much of the old thinking on the subject.

Hunter, a graduate of Indiana University, had lived among the impoverished as a social worker for eight and a half years. He knew their conditions firsthand. A man might be poor, said Hunter, not only when he was helpless but when he had a regular job and regular income. "Only the most miserable of them are starving or dependent on charity." The rest got no help from any source but were nonetheless in want. They had "too little of the common necessities to keep themselves at their best. . . ." They were ill-fed, ill-clad, and ill-sheltered. They were not, as many said, lazy or unfit; they just had no opportunity.

By Hunter's standard there were at least 10 million Americans in poverty during prosperous times, and perhaps as many as 15 or 20 million—an eighth to a quarter of the population. The vast

A young girl on New York's Lower East Side. (photograph by Jacob A. Riis, The Jacob A. Riis Collection, Museum of the City of New York)

majority of them were foreign-born. There were three to six times as many working poor as helpless poor.

According to the young social worker, the symptoms of poverty were not just dependency on others for survival. They also included child labor, disease, poor housing, accidents, illiteracy, unemployment, low wages. Surveys of this period show that it took at least $800 a year for a family to maintain itself at the lowest possible standard. But a study of 109,481 people in New York showed that one-half the workers earned $400 or less; one-eighth, $200 or less. The average weekly wage of women in 1905 was $5.25.

According to the 1900 census, 6½ million Americans—one-fourth of the labor force—had been unemployed at one time or another during the year. Of these, 2 million had been without jobs for as long as four to six months. Of the 606,000 inhabitants of Boston in 1902, 136,000 had to seek charity from public authorities alone. That same year 60,463 families in Manhattan were evicted from their tenements for nonpayment of rent. There was so much poverty that one of every ten New Yorkers who died had to be buried at public expense in a public cemetery, a potter's field.

The widespread nature of poverty in the Progressive Era made it inevitable that the downtrodden would react militantly to redress their wrongs. And react they did—in many ways.

13

The Progressives

On a cold, dreary Thursday, January 11, 1912, supervisors at the Everett Cotton Mill in Lawrence, Massachusetts, distributed pay envelopes to employees—a normal Thursday chore. But the reaction of women weavers, mostly Polish, who received the envelopes was not normal. As they counted their money they began shouting, "Short pay, not enough pay."

The Massachusetts legislature had recently reduced the legal workweek for women from fifty-six hours to fifty-four, and this was the first paycheck after the cut in hours went into effect. The women at Everett, like those throughout Lawrence, had expected they would get the same pay for fifty-four hours as for fifty-six, just as had happened when the workweek went down from fifty-eight hours to fifty-six. But the company this time refused to pay for the two hours, and pay envelopes thus were "short" an average of 32 cents.

Company officials talked to the women through an interpreter, trying to calm them. But the women sat at their machines and refused to work. By nightfall 1,750 had deserted their looms, and within a couple of days there were 25,000 textile workers on strike throughout Lawrence.

Lawrence, a city of 86,000, was a one-industry town, employing 32,000 workers in its cotton and woolen mills. Forty-eight percent of the population was foreign-born—from Poland, Italy, French Canada, Russia, Syria, Lithuania, and twenty other countries. The average wage was $8.76 a week for fifty-six hours. One-third of the employees earned $7 or less.

With these small wages, a worker had to pay $4 or $5 a week for a tenement flat—half or more of his pay. Sixty percent of the families took in boarders to help cover the rent. Wives and children were forced to work in order to make ends meet. Observers who studied Lawrence were agreed that the conditions of its people were lamentable. "The children went hungry," a witness told a committee of the United States Congress. "There were days when only bread and water kept them alive." Meat was a rarity. So was milk, at 7 cents a quart. Margaret Sanger, the famous birth-control advocate, said she had "never seen in any place children so ragged and so deplorable."

The 32-cent cut in weekly pay, therefore, was a last straw for Lawrence workers. Their strike, led by a radical group, the Industrial Workers of the World (IWW), was a bitter protest. During the stoppage 365 workers were arrested; 2 were killed and many injured by police and troops, 1,400 of which patrolled the city. After nine weeks the strike was won.

The Progressive Era saw a sharp escalation of labor struggles of this kind. In the mid-1890's there had been about 1,300 strikes a year. In 1903 the figure was 4,000. Some of them were incredibly severe. During the fifteen-month stoppage of miners in Cripple Creek, Colorado (1903–04), for example, 42 miners were killed, 112 wounded, 1,345 held in "bullpens," and 773 forcibly deported out of town. General Sherman Bell, who was in charge of the troops sent to Cripple Creek, said, "To hell with the Constitution. We're not following the Constitution."

Skilled and semiskilled workers tended to join the American Federation of Labor, which grew from 278,000 in 1898 to 1,676,000 in 1904. But the unskilled and foreign-born looked to the IWW and a few AFL unions that were socialist-controlled. The misery and hopes of these impoverished workers were captured in a song written by Ralph Chaplin, "Solidarity Forever":

It is we who plowed the prairies,
    built the cities where they trade;
Dug the mines and built the workshops;
    endless miles of railroads laid;
Now we stand outcast and starving,
    'mid the wonders we have made;
But the union makes us strong.

Also speaking for the poor those days was a growing socialist movement. The Socialist Party, formed in 1900–01, began with 4,536 members and increased to 117,984 by 1912. It published thirteen daily newspapers, eight of them in foreign languages. Eugene V. Debs, its candidate for President in 1912, polled 900,000 votes as against 6¼ million for President-elect Woodrow Wilson.

The intellectuals who supported the socialist movement included such well-known figures as the philosopher John Dewey, the economist and later United States Senator Paul Douglas, writ-

Meeting of coal mine strikers. (Library of Congress)

The great railway strikes. Above: Meat train leaving the Chicago stock-yards under escort of United States Cavalry, 1894. Below: Attack by strikers and their friends on scab switchmen and brakemen of the Chicago, Burlington & Quincy Railroad, 1888. (Library of Congress)

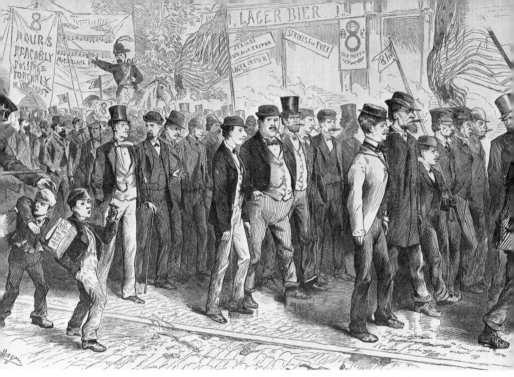

The eight-hours movement: procession of workingmen on strike in the Bowery. (Library of Congress)

ers Jack London and Floyd Dell, and the future newspaper columnist Walter Lippmann. The socialists, at their peak, were able to elect fifty-six mayors, one Congressman, and three hundred local aldermen. They organized unions, held meetings, and agitated for a socialist system in which the nation itself, rather than private individuals, would own the factories and banks. This, they said, was the only way to cure poverty.

Along with the radicals and the labor militants was another force crying out for the downtrodden. It was led by middle-class dissenters who favored reform of the system rather than revolution.

One group of dissenters sought to change the character of local government. Scores of cities and states were ruled by corrupt hacks who enriched themselves shamefully at public expense.

The progressives succeeded in ousting quite a few of them. Hazen S. Pingree, a wealthy shoe manufacturer, "threw the rascals out" in Detroit; Samuel H. Jones became mayor in Toledo; Tom L. Johnson in Cleveland; Seth Low in New York; Ben Lindsey in Denver; Joseph Folk in St. Louis—to name a few.

On the state level there were men such as Robert M. La Follette, who was elected governor of Wisconsin in 1900. A small, wiry man with iron-gray hair, La Follette was later a United States Senator and the most prominent liberal of his time. In 1924 he ran for President on a third-party ticket and received 5 million votes.

The political progressives campaigned for higher taxation of the railroads, the income tax, primary elections, women's suffrage, abolition of child labor, and similar planks.

A second group of dissenters were the muckrakers. They were the "Ralph Naders" of 1900–15. In hundreds of articles and books, they exposed a host of injustices. Lincoln Steffens wrote on corruption in the city of St. Louis; Ida Tarbell on the peculations of the Standard Oil Company; Ray Stannard Baker on the greed of the railroads; Samuel Hopkins Adams on patent medicines; David Graham Phillips on "the treason of the Senate." Upton Sinclair wrote in his novel *The Jungle,* about the disgraceful conditions in Chicago's packinghouses; it led to the famous Meat Inspection Act. Muckraking, in fact, was a necessary precursor to reforms that reached a peak in the first Wilson Administration.

Yet another force seeking to help the underdog was the social worker. The novelist Jack London said of social workers that "they do everything for the poor except get off their backs." But many of them did things to help the lower classes that the government was not yet willing to do. They organized nurseries, built playgrounds and kindergartens, taught English to immigrants, provided relief for those in want, and performed a dozen other services. Perhaps the most famous social worker of her time was the founder of Chicago's Hull House, Jane Addams.

Ms. Addams' father was a leading banker, miller, and state senator in Stephenson County, Illinois, where she was born. Though frail in health, she had no worries for the future insofar as money was concerned. But like so many other young persons of similar circumstances, she was troubled by a sense of emptiness, purposelessness.

She recalled how as a child of seven she had visited the slums of Freeport, near her hometown. She promised herself then "that when I grow up I should, of course, have a large house, but it would not be built around the other large houses, but right in the midst of horrid little houses like these." On one of her trips abroad, while sitting in a cathedral in Ulm, Germany, the idea came to her that she too should build a cathedral. It would not be for worship, "but a cathedral of humanity, a place where beauty, in its broadest sense, could be brought into the lives of the poor and lowly."

Jane Addams did not have to build her cathedral in a slum. She was given a big house and land on Halsted Street in Chicago which she converted into a settlement house.

Hull House—named after the man who donated the property —sponsored classes in English; formed clubs for young people; trained men and women in technical crafts; held discussions on literary subjects; organized singing, gym, and other activities; provided a library; and gave shelter to working girls who needed a home. Most important, it prodded the authorities for reform.

The Hull House founder, for instance, prevailed on the city to establish the first juvenile court. Here young delinquents were treated not as hardened criminals—as in previous times—but with the leniency due first offenders. When the settlement learned that children in its area were paid 4 cents an hour for sewing garments, it lobbied for an antisweatshop bill. It exposed the unsanitary conditions under which milk was sold from large metal cans.

Almost any human problem, large or small, attracted Jane Addams' attention. Once she petitioned the city to do something about the uncollected garbage and the stinking sewers on the West Side. With the help of the newspapers, she was appointed garbage inspector, and rose at six A.M. to follow the wagons and see that the garbage was collected.

The West Side was then a hellhole of vice and corruption, containing 255 saloons, and ruled by Alderman Johnny Powers. Jane Addams tried three times to unseat Powers. She agitated for prison reform; she joined with the National Child Labor Committee to win a shorter workday and a minimum wage for chil-

Jane Addams. (Library of Congress)

dren; she crusaded for workmen's compensation for employees injured on the job; and she served four years on the Chicago School Board. As a feminist she worked for women's suffrage, and as a pacifist she became president of the Women's International League for Peace and Freedom. In 1931 she was awarded a Nobel Peace Prize.

Taking each act or campaign on its own, Jane Addams' life seems remarkably unfocused. But social workers then lived with the hope that if they could plant the seed of human concern in one small place it would spread everywhere. Let the nation pass a reform bill on child labor, for instance, and the mood would continue until many other needed reforms were passed and America became a land without poverty.

It didn't come out that way, but that was the social worker's dream.

Whatever their shortcomings, the social workers, muckrakers, and political progressives did make an impact on American life. Historian Arthur M. Schlesinger, Sr., points out that there were more reforms on behalf of the common man in the first fifteen years of the twentieth century "than in all previous American history."

The men in power in Washington were forced to listen to all this agitation—and do something about it.

The shift in sentiment first became apparent in the Administration of Theodore Roosevelt. "Teddy" Roosevelt became President on September 14, 1901, when President McKinley died of a wound inflicted in Buffalo by a boyish-looking anarchist.

At the time, Roosevelt, a hero of the Spanish-American War, was known as an archconservative. He had been born to an upperclass New York family, was educated at Harvard, and entered politics at the age of twenty-three. As a state representative he denounced a bill granting a shorter workday for streetcar workers as "socialistic and un-American." He opposed pensions for teachers and praised President Cleveland for suppressing the national railroad strike of 1894. The way to handle radicals, he said, was to take "ten or a dozen of their leaders out, standing . . . them against a wall and shooting them dead."

But the country was in a mood for change, and Teddy Roosevelt changed with the country. He gained a reputation for resisting big business when he settled the anthracite miners' strike of 1902. The 150,000 coal diggers had been out five months when Roosevelt told the mine owners that if they didn't agree to arbitrate the dispute he would send in 10,000 soldiers to operate the mines. This was a new attitude for a Chief Executive. Other Presidents, such as Cleveland, had used troops to *smash* strikes. Roosevelt threatened to use them to cool off the corporations.

Women's dormitory, Kings County Alms House, Brooklyn. (photograph by Byron, Byron Collection, Museum of the City of New York)

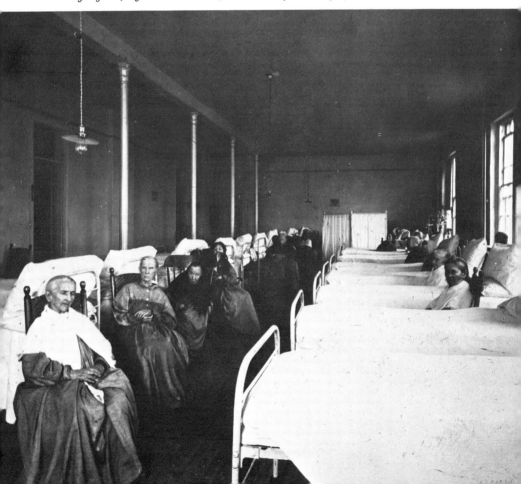

Roosevelt's image as a progressive was further enhanced when he prosecuted a big holding company—Northern Securities—in 1903–04. This company controlled three big railroads—the Northern Pacific, the Great Northern, and the Chicago, Burlington & Quincy. Roosevelt had it dissolved. In his seven and a half years in office, "Teddy" entered twenty-five indictments against monopolies, including the sugar and beef trusts. He prosecuted Standard Oil and secured a $29 million fine against it.

During that period, too, a law was passed to give more power to the Interstate Commerce Commission, which regulated railroads. Another banned harmful drugs and chemicals in food, liquor, and medicine. The hours of work for trainmen were reduced, and railroad workers won a reform they had demanded for a long time: a new law providing that in case of accident, workers were to get compensation whether the accident was their own fault or the company's. Previously they had to prove in court that it was management's fault; otherwise they received nothing.

The next President, William Howard Taft, took the mood of reform a little further—though not as far as the dissenters wanted. He instituted twice as many antitrust prosecutions as Roosevelt. Under his guidance, Congress passed a law establishing postal savings banks, making it easier for the poor to save money. A Sixteenth Amendment to the Constitution gave Congress the right to pass a graduated income tax. Laws were approved setting safety standards for mines and railroads. An eight-hour day was enacted for government workers.

Meanwhile the reform spirit was also at work at the state level. By 1912 thirty-eight states had passed laws restricting child labor. Twenty-eight states established maximum limits on hours of work for women. Workmen's compensation bills were enacted guaranteeing an injured laborer compensation for accident—again, whether the accident was the fault of management or his own carelessness.

Little by little, government assumed greater responsibility for the welfare of the average person—something it had refused to do in the nineteenth century.

The peak of the progressive mood came with the election of

Woodrow Wilson in 1912. Wilson was the son of a Presbyterian minister, a college professor, historian, and president of Princeton University. Like Roosevelt he was also a conservative before he took office. He sided with the coal companies in the 1902 anthracite strike, and protested the levying of fines against big corporations. But he too moved with the tide.

Under Wilson's rule the Clayton Anti-Trust Act authorized more vigorous prosecution of the monopolies; it also exempted labor unions from being prosecuted as trusts—a favorite method used by courts to end strikes. More important still were a host of social bills. Wilson signed into law the graduated income tax, introduced by a young congressman from Tennessee, Cordell Hull. The theory behind the income tax was that taxes should fall heaviest on those who could afford to pay them. In this first income tax bill the levy ranged from 1 percent on incomes of $3,000 and $4,000, to a maximum of 6 percent on earnings of $500,000 or more. In succeeding years the percentages at both the bottom and the top became much higher.

Under Wilson, too, the abysmal conditions under which merchant sailors worked were improved; a limit of eight hours was set on the workday of railroad employees; child labor was further restricted; a workmen's compensation bill was passed for federal employees; and easier credit was provided for farmers. With passage of the Federal Farm Loan Act, twelve federal land banks were empowered to sell bonds to the public and use the money for loans to farmers at interest rates of 5 to 6 percent.

All in all, there seemed to be greater concern for the injured and oppressed during the Progressive Era. After a decade and a half, the middle-class reformers could point to a considerable enrichment of American life. The slums remained, it is true. But a network of parks, schools, playgrounds, roads, and sewerage systems surrounded them to make urban living more tolerable. There were 3½ million automobiles on the highways by 1916, and gaslight was rapidly giving way to electricity. Real wages were only slightly higher than in 1913, but at least they were not plunging downward. Soon, spurred by war, they would go up some more, and almost half of the workers would be working a shorter workweek of forty-eight hours.

Yet, the balance between rich and poor remained in disarray—and in half a generation would become worse. Statistics for 1917 show that only 1½ million families (out of 21 million) earned enough money to pay income tax. On the other hand, the number of millionaires had risen from 7,509 in 1914 to 19,103—and would soon rise still more. The prosperity on the farm, two decades old, was about to be washed away by another cycle of overproduction.

Taken together, the package of regulatory and welfare measures neither checked the advance of unbridled wealth nor gave the poor a cushion against economic insecurity. The poor would have to wait two decades for more meaningful measures. Meanwhile the nation would experience the worst onrush of poverty it had ever known.

14

The Great Depression

In the dozen years after the United States entered World War I, a growing number of people came to believe that poverty was going out of style. President Calvin Coolidge stated in late 1928 that "the country is in the midst of an era of prosperity more extensive . . . than it has ever before experienced." A half year later Herbert Hoover, who followed Coolidge to the White House, exuberantly noted, "We in America are nearer to the final triumph over poverty than ever before in our land. The poorhouse is vanishing from among us."

A couple of months later the house caved in. The worst depression in United States history had begun.

Few people, however, could see that depression coming. According to the widely acclaimed economist Irving Fisher, the wartime affluence and the "golden twenties" had established "a permanently high plateau" of prosperity. It would last, presumably, forever—getting better all the time.

The economy had begun its prosperous climb with the outbreak of war in Europe in 1914. In the next five years the United States sold mountains of supplies to the embattled Europeans. So great was the demand for American products that by 1917 exports exceeded imports by $3½ billion. The export of steel quadrupled, that of wheat tripled, that of explosives jumped by 125 times.

The American farmer could hardly satisfy the demand for his produce. He was constantly trying to buy or rent more land to put into crops—and the prices he received soared precipitously. Cotton, selling for 8½ cents a pound in 1917, shot up to a record 36 cents by 1920; wheat zoomed from 97 cents a bushel to $2.73.

After the war there was a brief depression in 1921, when almost 5 million people were unemployed. For the next seven years, however, the economy continued its boom. The gross national product—the total amount of goods and services produced by the nation—was $70 billion in 1921, and $103 billion in 1929.

Anyone could see the change just by looking around at the automobiles on the road and the radios in the home. Only 7 million horseless carriages, as automobiles were called, were on the highways in 1920; there were 24 million of them nine years later. The number of radios sold increased by forty times from 1921 to 1929. There were other wonders to behold and savor: silent movies and then the talking pictures; electricity in the home, replacing gas and kerosene; new electrical appliances; the beginnings of air flight. Almost anything now could be bought on the installment plan, and workers were going into debt, confident that prosperity would last forever.

As the song of the day put it, "Happy Days Are Here Again."

From 1926 to 1929 prices on the stock market more than doubled. John D. Rockefeller, Jr., was earning so much money, his *income tax* alone was $6,278,000; Henry Ford and his son Edsel paid $5,100,000 income tax.

To be sure, there was still plenty of poverty around. If you defined poverty as a yearly income of $2,000 or less per family, there were at least 10 million such families—40 million or more people. The respected Brookings Institution placed the figure much higher: three-fifths of the nation. This was a serious indictment of the golden twenties. Yet there were 4 million fewer poor families than a few years back.

Suddenly—at least it seemed suddenly—the country was consumed by depression. There had been disturbing notes, even during the period of prosperity. At the height of the boom, one-fifth of the country's machines and equipment were idle—despite the fact that 2 million workers had no jobs. There was already a slump in shipbuilding, bituminous mining, textiles, and part of the iron and steel industry.

Above all, after the war agriculture had again fallen into a depressed state and had not recovered throughout most of the golden twenties. "Everyone seems to be prosperous and making money," said Senator George W. Norris of Nebraska, "except the farmer." With the end of the war, demand slackened. A bushel of wheat, selling for $2½ in 1917, was down to $1 two years later; pigs at 15 cents a pound fell to 7 cents; horses that had brought $200 each "could hardly be disposed of in 1922 at fifty dollars." That old devil, overproduction, again held the farmer in viselike grip. Total land value fell from $79 billion in 1920 to $58 billion in 1927, and somewhere between 1 and 2 million farm families deserted their land.

All this was a prelude to October 24, 1929—"Black Thursday." On that day the New York stock market took a sharp plunge downward. Five days later the prices of securities tumbled even further. A share of General Electric stock fell $47; that of American Telephone and Telegraph $34. "Stock prices virtually collapsed," reported *The New York Times*. It was "the most disastrous trading day in the stock market's history." The average price of the fifty leading stocks fell nearly $40—in just one day.

The economic decline that followed the crash was shocking. From October 1, 1929, to August 31, 1932, 4,835 banks failed. Hundreds of thousands of families lost $3¼ billion—many of them their life savings. The despair was typified by a woman in a Midwestern town who "beat with her fists upon the closed plate-glass doors and screamed and sobbed without restraint. She had in a savings account the $2,000 from her husband's insurance and $963 she had saved over a period of twenty-five years from making rag rugs." She ended up in an insane asylum a few days later.

The value of all stocks listed on the New York exchange fell from $90 billion to $16 billion. By late 1932 industrial production had fallen by one-half, construction by six-sevenths. Farm prices, already depressed, continued to drop, and a million more rural families abandoned their homesteads.

Wherever one turned, there was a wasteland of shattered lives. By March 1931 there were 4 million out of work, a year later 8 million; and when Franklin Roosevelt took office in March 1933, 13 million—by official figures. Others estimated it at 16 or 17 million, with a similar number working only part time. As of 1934 there were still 2½ million workers who had not had a job for two years or more, and 6 million for at least a year.

Those still lucky enough to hold jobs had their pay cut by 20, 30, or more percent. The number of city inhabitants evicted from their apartments ran into many hundreds of thousands. "This depression," commented one economist, "has been far more severe than any of the twenty depressions that we have experienced in this country since 1790."

Expressed in human terms, the Great Depression was more bleak than the bare statistics. Wrote one citizen to Governor Pinchot of Pennsylvania:

My four motherless children and I, the father, are on the verge of freezing and starving. Being several months out of work, I have no money to buy coal, food or winter clothes for my school children. . . . The landlord attempts to evict me from his premises. Two of my children are ill. So please, Mr. Governor, be kind and render your assistance . . . please assist us from cold and hunger, Mr. Gov. Pinchot.

Another letter read:

There are nine of us in the family. My father is out of work for a couple of months and we haven't got a thing [to] eat in the house. Mother is getting $12 a month of the county. If mother don't get any more help we will have to starve to death. I am a little girl 10 years old.

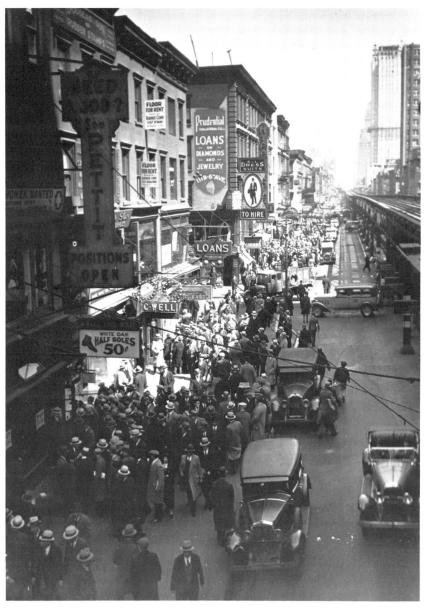

Crowds of unemployed waiting in front of employment agencies on Sixth Avenue, New York. (photograph by Byron, Byron Collection, Museum of the City of New York)

Shacks in New York housing unemployed people during the Depression. (photograph by Berenice Abbott for Federal Art Project "Changing New York," Museum of the City of New York)

According to the Department of Labor at least 200,000 waifs were wandering the land without means of support. President Herbert Hoover himself admitted there were "at least 10,000,000 deficient children in this country." One local hospital reported: "This week we have had four children admitted with the diagnosis of starvation. One who was found eating out of a garbage can, has died since admission."

In a single day in April 1932, Boston police picked up thirteen unidentified bodies, men who had died of hunger or committed suicide. At the city dump at 32nd Street and Cicero Avenue in

Chicago, large lines formed every day waiting to sift through the refuse as garbage trucks unloaded their waste.

While farmers were destroying cattle and crops that were unmarketable, police in dozens of towns reported items such as this one: "Attracted by smoke from the chimney of a supposedly empty summer cottage near Anwana Lake in Sullivan County, Constable Simon Glaser found a young couple starving. Three days without food, the wife, who is 23 years old, was hardly able to walk."

A check of Chicago schools in June 1931 revealed that "11,000 hungry children were being fed by teachers." The superintendent of schools sent an urgent plea to the governor of Illinois: "For God's sake, help us feed these children during the summer."

If there was one feature that lent a distinction of sorts to the Great Depression, it was that almost everyone suffered. It was no longer the urban immigrants or the working class or the farmers. Caught in the web was a majority of every class, including doctors, lawyers, engineers, professors, and businessmen. The man selling apples on the street corner was as likely to be a former certified public accountant as a drill press operator.

This was, future sociologists would say, a "majority" poverty. Forty-four-year-old Langlan Heinz, a man charged with vagrancy, told a Brooklyn court in May 1932 that he was a graduate of the University of Colorado and had held responsible jobs in China, Panama, and Venezuela as a civil engineer. But his resources were now depleted, and for the previous forty-six days he had been sleeping on a cot in a vacant lot near Flatbush Avenue. Housewives and schoolchildren in the neighborhood gave him food.

At least 10,000 college alumni were unemployed in New York alone, according to a *New York Times* estimate of July 27, 1932.

The glow of the 1920's faded. The tune of the day was no longer "Happy Days Are Here Again," but "Brother, Can You Spare a Dime?" In his 1930 play *The Green Pastures,* Marc Connelly summarized it well: "Everything nailed down is comin' loose."

President Hoover would not admit that the free enterprise system was "comin' loose." It was simply "readjusting"; prosperity, he said, was "just around the corner." To question "the basic strength of business," he said in November 1929, "is foolish."

Meanwhile, however, the Great Depression was gaining momentum, and everyone was crying for jobs and relief. The Communists called a national demonstration March 6, 1930, around the slogans, "Don't Starve—Fight" and "Work or Wages!" According to *The Daily Worker*, almost a million people in a dozen cities responded; there were 100,000 each in New York and Detroit.

Two months later another national protest brought out about a third as many as the first one, but it led to the formation of a Communist-controlled National Unemployed Council. Parallel to it, the Socialists established the Workers Alliance; and an unaffiliated radical, A. J. Muste, the National Unemployed League.

Before long the three groups—and many local ones—were conducting a guerrilla war against the depression, involving millions of people in small acts of resistance. They sat in at relief stations to demand aid; they demonstrated in front of city halls. Occasionally they raided a food warehouse or store. An Associated Press dispatch on January 20, 1931, from Oklahoma City reported: "A crowd of men and women, shouting that they were hungry and jobless, raided a grocery store near the City Hall today. Twenty-six of the men were arrested."

In 1932 a detachment of 20,000 World War I veterans, also Communist-led, bivouacked in front of the Capitol demanding early payment of a bonus promised them for 1945. Their placards read, "Heroes in 1917—Bums in 1932" and "We Fought for Democracy—What Did We Get?" Hoover sent General Douglas MacArthur and his aide, Major Dwight D. Eisenhower, to burn their camp down. Fifty-five people were injured.

The agitation on the farm was equally fierce. Not even the populist 1890's approached it in intensity, and certainly not in violence. A "Farmers' Holiday Association" in Iowa laid siege to Sioux City, Council Bluffs, and other cities in 1932. With guns, clubs, and fists the farmers declared themselves "on strike" to prevent milk and produce from reaching market. By holding back delivery, they thought they could force prices up. The effort failed, but it led to a nationwide movement throughout the farm states.

More successful was the campaign against foreclosures. When the New York Life Insurance Company tried to foreclose a farm in Cedar Rapids with a $30,000 mortage on it, the farmers prevented the sheriff from putting the farm for sale.

Often a forced sale was turned to the farmer's advantage. For example, the farm of Charles Grady of Champaign County, Illinois, with a $2,750 mortgage on it, was put on the block and "sold" for $4.75—no one dared bid any higher. Afterward it was given to Mr. Grady. An indebtedness of $1,200 on another farm was sold for $16.46. Tractors fell under the hammer for a quarter, horses for a dime, wagons for 15 cents. After the "sale" the property was leased free to its former owner for ninety-nine years.

No President could have disregarded the tempests of the 1930's. But Hoover's plan was first to help business—in the hope that some of that help would percolate down to the poor. Ironically, during a 1930 drought in Arkansas, he asked Congress to provide $45 million to save the animals but was displeased when senators added $20 million to feed human beings.

The "Great Engineer" was not exactly callous. He doubled the expenditures on public works such as Boulder Dam, and thereby created 600,000 jobs. But Hoover didn't feel the government should give the unemployed money for relief. They should either help themselves or rely on charity from such funds as the $175 million being raised by private businessmen for aid to the poor. The proposal in 1931 by Senator Robert M. La Follette, Jr., to use federal money to help the jobless was denounced as a "dole" and as an affront to the "dignity of the working man."

One self-help idea was thought up by an enterprising promoter of the International Apple Shippers' Association. The unemployed were given apples on credit, to be sold on street corners for a nickel apiece. Before long there were 6,000 men and women selling apples on New York's streets alone. Together with the breadline, this stood as the symbol of the Great Depression.

A comment on the economic progress of the Hoover Administration.
(drawing by Clifford Berryman, Library of Congress)

After the apple scheme someone thought up the "Give-a-Job" plan. Neighbors who still were working were asked to give a job to someone unemployed—to clean a yard, whitewash a cellar, or something of the sort. Another fashion in relief was "block aid": dwellers in the same block made weekly contributions for less fortunate friends.

None of this did much good. By 1931–32 it was clear that voluntarism was a failure, and public relief by local authorities had all but collapsed. A director of Jewish Social Research in New York told Congress in 1932: "Relief has been continuously and gradually reduced so that whole families are getting an average of $2.39 a week relief in New York City, with $3 and $4 and at the most $5 a week . . . in other cities."

There were 700,000 jobless in Chicago—40 percent of the labor force. But the city did not have the money to pay its teachers, let alone its paupers. New York, Detroit, Boston, and Philadelphia were similarly at the brink of bankruptcy. Niles, Ohio, reported it was supplying food to one-fourth of its population, 4,377 people, at 1½ cents a meal; and Tulsa, Oklahoma, announced a charity ration costing 6 cents per day per person. To prove how meagerly a person could live, the mayor of Syracuse put himself on a 9-cents-a-day diet for one week.

It was an intolerable situation. But Hoover rebuffed all efforts by Senator La Follette, Congressman Fiorello La Guardia, and others to introduce national relief sponsored by Washington. His major relief program, instead, was the Reconstruction Finance Corporation. Passed in January 1932, the RFC bill provided $3½ billion for loans to banks, insurance companies, and similar institutions to help them ward off disaster. Cynics called it a "breadline for big business." One of those that received a handsome handout on this breadline—$90 million—was a large Chicago bank once headed by former Vice-President Charles G. Dawes. By strange happenstance, Dawes was president of the RFC.

Almost as an afterthought, a rider was attached to the RFC bill granting $300 million in loans to the states—to be used for poor relief. An allocation of $300 million for relief, as against $3½ *billion* for the "breadline for big business"!

Obviously, with such an approach to the worst depression in American history there was little possibility of improving things. The month Franklin D. Roosevelt replaced Hoover, there were more people unemployed and more banks going broke than at any time in the past.

15

The First New Deal

"I pledge you, I pledge myself," Franklin Delano Roosevelt told the 1932 Democratic Party Convention, "to a new deal for the American people." The catchy phrase, soon on everyone's lips, came from a remark by Mark Twain's Connecticut Yankee: when out of a thousand men, six can crack the whip over the other 994, it is time for the "dupes" to seek a "new deal." Roosevelt, a tall, handsome, boyishly exuberant man with an exciting inflection to his voice, used such phrases with the instinct of an evangelist.

Unlike Hoover, who was a self-made man, Roosevelt was born well-to-do. His family tree on the paternal side was American back to the 1640's, when Claes Martenszen Van Roosevelt came to Nieuw Amsterdam from Holland. On his mother's side it went back to 1621, when the French-Dutch Delano family (originally De La Noye) set foot in Plymouth. Genealogists claim he was distantly related to eleven American Presidents—including Teddy Roosevelt, his fifth cousin.

Young Franklin, an only son, was educated by governesses and tutors, had his own pony and sailboat, and was taken to Europe eight times before he had learned how to shave properly. He studied at the best schools—Groton, Harvard, Columbia Law

School—and lived well. Nonetheless, Roosevelt was no hidebound conservative. His liberalism was enriched by marriage to Eleanor Roosevelt—niece of Teddy—who was more advanced in her social views than Franklin. As a state senator in New York he made a good, though not remarkable, record as a progressive.

Roosevelt supported Wilson in the 1912 elections and served subsequently as Assistant Secretary of the Navy. In 1921 he was chosen as vice-presidential candidate on the Democratic ticket. He fell into obscurity after August 1921, when he contracted infantile paralysis. For the rest of his life he wore braces on his legs and had difficulty moving about.

It says something for Roosevelt's personal courage that he overcame this handicap. Urged on by Eleanor and by his close friend Louis Howe, he ran for governor of New York in 1928 and was elected. Four years later he challenged Hoover for the Presidency and administered a humiliating defeat on an incumbent President: he won by 472 electoral votes to 59.

"FDR," as he was often referred to, was a warm, likable man, with a delightful smile. He was an excellent mixer, and charmingly impulsive. Yet, as columnist Walter Lippmann observed, he was neither a tribune of the people nor a crusader at heart. What distinguished him was flexibility. "It is common sense," he told students at Oglethorpe University, "to take a method and try it. If it fails, admit it frankly and try another. But above all, try something."

At his inauguration on Saturday, March 4, 1933, FDR told the American people that "the only thing we have to fear is fear itself."

Earlier that morning Governor Herbert H. Lehman of New York had closed the banks in his state—to prevent a run by depositors to take out their money. Since more than a quarter of the nation's savings institutions had failed, many people preferred to put their dollars under a mattress rather than keep them in the bank. Nine other states, including Michigan and California, had declared bank holidays before New York.

On the fateful morning of FDR's inauguration, too, the New

York Stock Exchange announced it was shutting down, as did the Chicago Board of Trade and a half dozen commodity markets. The economic machine seemed to be grinding to a shuddering halt.

On Sunday, Roosevelt invoked the old Trading with the Enemy Act to forbid the export of gold or trade in foreign money. The President also ordered every bank in the nation to suspend business for the next four days. Whether he had the right to do this under the law is not clear; but as humorist Will Rogers later said, the whole country was with FDR even if he did wrong—so long as he did something. "If he burned down the Capitol," said Rogers, "we would cheer and say, 'Well, we at least got a fire started anyhow.' "

The bank holiday was followed by the famous "One Hundred Days"—the most hectic 100 days of legislation ever produced by the United States Congress. After passing some hasty bills to provide help for the banks, Congress turned to the next patient —the sickest one of all—the unemployed.

The professors whom Roosevelt enlisted to draft the novel plans for the New Deal were called the "Brain Trust." The Brain Trust prescription for the jobless—as expressed by Roosevelt's right-hand man, Harry L. Hopkins—was to "feed the hungry, and Goddamn fast." To feed the hungry, the New Deal secured legislation to set up the Federal Emergency Relief Administration (FERA). An outlay of $500 million was allocated for the FERA— to begin with—and Hopkins was chosen to head it. He was the kind of maverick Roosevelt liked—buoyant, earthy, and outspoken.

Within two hours, while workmen were still remodeling an office for him and his desk was in the hallway, "Skinny" Hopkins gave away $5 million. Within a day he had made grants to seven states. Where Hoover had grudgingly allocated $300 million in loans, Hopkins, in two and a half years, disbursed $3 billion in nonrepayable grants. The money went to the states, and from there to cities and counties, which dispensed it to the poor. At its peak in February 1934, the FERA program was paying 70 percent of national relief costs and providing help for 8 million families—28 million people.

Harry L. Hopkins. (photograph by Harris and Ewing, Library of Congress)

Hopkins, in addition, proclaimed three principles of public welfare which made old charity workers blink. Federal relief, he announced, was not an act of charity but a direct obligation of the government; the citizen was entitled to it as a matter of right, not gift. Secondly, he called for cash payments rather than grocery chits; the recipient himself made the decision on how to spend the money. Finally, he insisted that relief must include funds not only for food but for rent, clothing, and medical care. Radicals criticized the program as inadequate; conservatives sneered at it as a dole.

As an offshoot of the FERA, Hopkins and his assistants sketched a national plan for "made work." The Civil Works Administration (CWA) initiated 180,000 projects within four months—to repair schools, clean playgrounds, improve roads, beautify parks, and operate a pest and erosion control program. The criterion for each project was not how useful it was in the long run, but how quickly it could create temporary jobs in the winter of 1933–34. Through the next few years the CWA made work for 4 million unemployed, half of whom, for one reason or another, were not eligible for direct relief.

Another alphabetical agency that made jobs was the Public Works Administration (PWA), headed by an old-time progressive, Harold L. Ickes. The purpose here was to revive the construction industry, rather than find temporary work for those in want. But of course it did create jobs—a half million of them. When the PWA was phased out during World War II, it had spent $4 billion on 34,000 projects, among them the Tennessee Valley Authority; the Triborough Bridge and the Lincoln Tunnel in New York; the port of Brownsville, Texas; and innumerable sewerage systems, city auditoriums, schools, and hospitals.

The PWA also constructed fifty airports, thousands of miles of strategic highways, the aircraft carriers *Yorktown* and *Enterprise,* and a host of submarines, destroyers, airplanes, and light cruisers. One of the PWA's innovations, though on a small scale, was slum clearance and public housing. In four and a half years it built 25,000 dwelling units for lower-class families.

The New Deal also initiated a number of special programs for young people. Through the Civilian Conservation Corps, from 1933 to 1941 more than 2½ million youth were put to work in camps run by the War Department, at $30 a month and board. Those who wanted to continue their schooling were given monthly stipends or part-time work by the National Youth Administration.

The vast expenditures for relief and jobs were something new —a sharp departure from the American past. The federal government replaced local governments and local charity as the primary agency for alleviating hunger and want. And it did it without worrying too much about a balanced budget. It was willing to go heavily into debt, in other words, to "feed the hungry, and Goddamn fast."

This, too, was a new idea in government circles. The theory of previous Administrations had been that Washington should not spend more money each year than what it collected in taxes. Every year from 1920 through 1930, in fact, there was a budget surplus. But every year under Roosevelt there was a deficit. The national debt grew larger and larger.

Economists of the 1930's, following the theories of John Maynard Keynes of Britain, believed in something called "compensatory spending." The worst thing in the world, they said, was not a budget deficit but a sick economy. In bad times, therefore, the government should compensate for the loss of consumer buying power by pumping money into the economy. That would get things rolling again. Then, when times improved, the government could raise taxes to pay off part of the debt, as well as to prevent the economy from moving ahead too fast. It was a complicated theory, but it provided the general principle under which the United States and all Western governments have functioned ever since.

Relief and "made" jobs revived hope and stopped matters from getting worse. But the central problem was still recovery—how to get privately owned factories and farms back to normal production.

There were two schools of thought within the New Deal on this. One held that what the nation needed was a planned economy. Its leading exponent was economist Rexford G. Tugwell, the Assistant Secretary of Agriculture. The other school said that what was needed was social reform, such as unemployment compensation, and much stronger antitrust action. If the government would break up the big monopolies, real compe-

Houses in a black district in Atlanta, 1936. (photograph by Walker Evans, Library of Congress)

tition could return and the economy could recover without central planning.

Roosevelt supported the "planners" in what historians have called the "First New Deal"; then shifted, a few years later, to the trustbusters in the "Second New Deal."

A planned economy, of course, was what communists and socialists advocated. But many liberals and even some businessmen believed that a planned economy was possible—even necessary—under capitalism. Among them were Charles A. Beard, George Soule, Senator Robert M. La Follette, Jr.—to name a few. The list also included Gerard Swope, president of General Electric Company.

What Tugwell proposed was to group businessmen into national associations, one for each industry. Each association would determine how much should be produced by its industry, would set prices, and agree on common trade practices, personnel policies, and similar matters. To coordinate the planning of the various associations, there would be a "Central Industrial Integration Board," run by the government. It would have the power to overrule or modify any of the association plans.

Roosevelt, however, refused to go quite that far toward central planning. The result was a watered-down version of the Tugwell scheme. Under a law passed in June 1933, the National Recovery Administration (NRA) was set up to help businessmen draw up "codes of fair practices" for each industry. Those codes dealt with wages, hours, prices, selling techniques, and exchange of information. In effect, the Administration pledged that if industry raised wages and reduced hours, it would be allowed collectively to increase prices without being subject to antitrust prosecution.

The man appointed to head the NRA was General Hugh Johnson. A gruff, blustering man—though not without charm—he threw himself into the job with the energy of a lion. First results, however, were not encouraging. Of the ten major industries asked to draft codes, only one responded quickly—cotton textile. Textile firms agreed to eliminate child labor, raise wages, cut hours, and bargain with unions; in return they were allowed to limit cotton production and thereby raise prices.

Other industries, however, dragged their feet. Johnson therefore introduced a blanket code for *all* industry—until specific codes could be written. Under the blanket code, the workweek for blue collar workers was cut to thirty-five hours, and for white collar workers to forty hours. The former were to be paid a 40-cents-an-hour minimum wage, the latter 30 to 37½ cents an hour ($12 to $15 a week).

Since the blanket code was not enforceable by law, Johnson set about to have it enforced by public opinion. Every company that agreed to carry out the code was given a placard showing a big blue eagle and the slogan, "We Do Our Part." Consumers were urged to buy only those goods that displayed the "Blue Eagle," and boycott those that didn't. President Roosevelt "sold" the Blue Eagle in talks over the radio, and Johnson organized parades to win support for it. Within a short time 2¼ million companies joined the Blue Eagle campaign. Only a small number of businessmen held out, the most important being Henry Ford.

Prodded by the Blue Eagle drive, individual branches of business were soon drafting their own codes of fair practices. All

Cartoon depicting the Blue Eagle campaign. (drawing by Clifford Berryman, Library of Congress)

told, under Johnson and his successor, Donald Richberg, 576 basic and 189 supplementary codes were drawn up and approved. After a year of operation the NRA could boast that hourly wages in manufacture had gone up 31 percent, and weekly earnings—despite a cut in the workweek—14 percent.

On the minus side, however, there was an explosion of complaints about price-fixing and the fact that many small companies were driven out of business. Theoretically the codes were to be written with the participation of the whole business community —large and small—as well as that of labor, the consumer, and the government. In practice it was the legal experts of big business who did the drafting. They wrote provisions on prices, trade practices, and production that helped the larger firms but pushed quite a few smaller ones into bankruptcy. Clarence Darrow, the famous civil liberties attorney who made a study of this problem for Roosevelt, was so disgusted that he urged the President to socialize industry and have done with it.

At the same time there was a big hue and cry against the NRA from labor. To appease the unions, the bill setting up the NRA had included a section guaranteeing the right of labor to organize into unions and bargain collectively. But this plan wasn't working at all. Employers in unorganized industries simply refused to abide—and there was no machinery to enforce the law. Workers began to call the NRA the "National Run Around."

The NRA was taunted from all sides—left, right, and center. Herbert Hoover called it "fascism, pure fascism." The Communists echoed the sentiment in a derogatory pamphlet they published about the "fascist Blue Eagle." Even Harry Hopkins told Johnson: "Hugh, your codes stink." Tugwell was distraught because he had hoped that government, not business, would have the decisive voice in running the economy.

The undoing of the Blue Eagle turned out to be a chicken. In February 1935 Roosevelt asked Congress to extend the recovery act for another two years. But while Congress was deliberating, the Supreme Court in May 1935 handed down a decision in the Schechter case.

The Schechter brothers were poultry jobbers in Brooklyn who

had been charged with selling diseased chickens and with paying chicken killers lower wages than provided in the Live Poultry Code. The court ruled with the Schechters. It said that the NRA had no right to regulate industry in any way, and that the law was unconstitutional. "America Stunned," read a headline in the *London Daily Express*. "Roosevelt's Two Years' Work Killed in Twenty Minutes."

While the NRA was trying to cure the sickness of industry, the New Deal had another plan for agriculture. In a sense, the plan was absolutely weird. Though millions were on relief or the CWA, Secretary of Agriculture Henry A. Wallace ordered the slaughter of 6 million little pigs and 200,000 sows. During the first year of agricultural planning, the government also paid $100 million to cotton farmers to plow under 10 million acres of their crop. Forever after, the image of killing pigs and plowing under cotton and grain was fixed in many American minds as the image of the New Deal.

Yet there were millions of people starving on fertile farms because they had produced too many hogs and too much grain or cotton, forcing their prices downward. The cotton crop was expected to be so big that year, there would be a 16-million-bale surplus, and a consequent decline in price of catastrophic proportion. Twenty-two thousand government agents, most of them volunteers, descended on the cotton area, therefore, to offer farmers $6 to $20 an acre for plowing up one-quarter of the acres under seed.

With the hog market also in despair, payments were made to compensate for the slaughter of the pigs. Wallace conceded it was "a shocking commentary on our civilization" to kill animals and plow under farm produce. But it was no worse, he said, than plowing workers out of the factories.

The planned scarcity in the farm sections proceeded in a more orderly fashion after 1933, with the emphasis on taking acreage out of cultivation—the "domestic allotment" plan. The Agricultural Adjustment Administration (AAA) determined how many acres of each commodity should be withdrawn from planting.

Committees selected by the farmers in every county then made allotments, based on how many acres had been planted by the individual farmer in previous years. The system was meant to produce a price that "would give agricultural commodities a purchasing power" equivalent to what was enjoyed in the base period—August 1909 to July 1914. This was called "parity."

The AAA, or Triple-A, was supplemented by another alphabetical agency—the Commodity Credit Corporation (CCC). The CCC offered loans to farmers at higher than the market price. Suppose that cotton was selling at 9 cents a pound. A farmer could bring his cotton to the CCC warehouse and be given a loan of, say, 10 cents a pound. Later he could either redeem the loan or let the CCC keep his cotton. This plan too was designed to raise farm prices.

Statistics showed that the Triple-A and CCC increased rural purchasing power by one-third in a single year. There were harmful side effects, of course, that blurred this glowing picture. Many landlords, for instance, simply cut the acreage for their tenants and sharecroppers—forcing hundreds of thousands to give up farming. Within a few years there were a million uprooted farm families—like the Okies described in John Steinbeck's *The Grapes of Wrath*.

With all that, however, the New Deal saved agriculture from a much worse fate. Even John T. Flynn, a right-wing critic of Roosevelt, admitted in 1940 that "very obviously the farmer's condition is improved." Income was higher, and the number of farms with electricity had risen from 13 to 33 percent.

16

The Second New Deal

When Roosevelt first took office, conditions were so bad almost everyone was willing to give him a free hand. He could have proclaimed himself economic czar, or nationalized the banks, or introduced a planned economy; the nation was ready to try virtually anything to climb out of its despair.

After a year of the First New Deal, however, the critics began to attack it with increasing ferocity. By 1934 the economic situation was improving, and Roosevelt was under pressure from both right and left. Conservatives said he had gone too far; he had upset the free enterprise system. Radicals and many liberals said he hadn't gone far enough.

Social workers, for instance, criticized Roosevelt for leaving the dispensation of relief in the hands of local governments, each of which had different rules and different pay schedules. If you lived in one town, you might get considerably more than in another. In one place you might be eligible for relief, in another you weren't. The whole system was obviously unfair. There should be, said the social workers, a single relief plan administered by the federal government. Roosevelt probably agreed with this, but before everything else he was a "practicing politician." He didn't want to offend thousands of local political figures who objected to having control of relief taken out of their hands. The relief system therefore remained unchanged—much as it had been in the seventeenth, eighteenth, and nineteenth centuries.

This same tendency to compromise between opposing interests caused other problems. Millions of jobless now had temporary jobs or were on welfare. But their status was still unenviable—wages were too low, relief inadequate, too many people were excluded. The three major organizations of unemployed, therefore, continued and even increased their protests.

Hardly a relief station or city hall was immune from picket lines and sit-ins. There were literally thousands of small demonstrations against the eviction of families who couldn't pay their rent. Here is a report of one of them in a radical paper of May 1, 1934:

> "This constable is for sale. How much is the bid? Sold for 8 cents." The Pennsylvania Unemployed League in Pittsburgh sold the constable at a mass eviction fight. The eviction was stopped by a mass demonstration. When leaving the house, "an accident" occurred to the constable and landlord. They went to the hospital. "Who threw the bricks?" Shrugged shoulders was the reply. No more evictions for six months.

The actions of the unemployed blended with an eruption of strikes by blue collar workers. There were five times as many strikers in 1934 as during the last year of Hoover's administration. The nationwide strike of 475,000 textile workers brought 11,000 national guardsmen to the mill towns. Ten unionists were killed, hundreds injured. On the West Coast, a colorful Australian, Harry Bridges, led a strike that tied up the ports for months. In Toledo, the unemployed defied a court order and helped the Electric Auto-Lite workers win the first big union victory in the automobile industry. In Minneapolis, flying squads of pickets roamed the streets like revolutionary militia. They won three big victories in trucking and related industries. Not since 1919 had there been such ferment in labor's ranks.

Franklin Roosevelt remained immensely popular personally.

But he was being pecked at by progressives, radicals, and rightists in a way he could not ignore. Moreover, millions were still jobless; the depression was by no means over.

Minnesota Governor Floyd Olson stated that unless capitalism could find a cure for depression, "I hope the present system of government goes right down to hell." Olson suggested that the "key industries" should be taken over and run by the government. What the country needed, he said, was a "Cooperative Commonwealth."

In California, the old muckraker Upton Sinclair organized EPIC (End Poverty in California). He proposed to end poverty by establishing rural communes where people lived together, worked together, and shared things in common. He would also set up a system of leased factories where the workers produced goods for use, not for profits.

EPIC was so popular that when Sinclair ran in the Democratic primary for governor of California in 1934, he defeated New Dealer George Creel by 436,000 votes to 288,000. The author of the famous novel *The Jungle* was defeated in the November elections only because the New Dealers supported a conservative Republican against him.

Almost any panacea, whether put forth sincerely or demagogically, could find an audience of hundreds of thousands. A sixty-seven-year-old doctor, Francis Townsend, formed Old Age Revolving Pensions, Limited, in January 1934. It demanded a government pension of $200 a month for everyone over sixty, provided the pensioner agreed to spend the money within that month. The organization boasted 1,200 clubs before the end of the year and secured between 10 and 25 million signatures for its pension petition.

The silver-tongued priest Father Charles Coughlin, whose radio addresses drew audiences of 30 to 40 million each week, formed the National Union for Social Justice. Coughlin said that capitalism was dead. He denounced bankers, and urged something akin to Mussolini's corporate state in Italy. Millions flocked to this banner too.

The most serious concern for Roosevelt, because they were so politically minded, was the 27,000 "Share Our Wealth" clubs inspired by Senator Huey ("Kingfish") Long of Louisiana. Share Our Wealth claimed 7½ million sympathizers. Old Huey, a demagogue with fascist leanings, was a rabble-rouser of worrisome dimensions. With mussed red hair and an angelic round face, he could bring any crowd to its feet when he called for confiscating all individual wealth above a certain amount and dividing it among the poor.

Huey's slogans—"Share Our Wealth," "Every Man a King"— rang with a certain credibility; and his rubelike pose had enormous appeal, especially to farmers. Huey promised that in "my first days in the White House" he would appoint John D. Rockefeller, Jr., and Andrew Mellon to give away their own and other fortunes so that every "deserving family" would have enough for a car, a home, a radio, and a good livelihood. If it was weak economics, it was strong propaganda—enough to give New Dealers the jitters. A poll taken by the Democratic National Committee indicated that the Kingfish would get 3 to 4 million votes as a third-ticket presidential candidate—enough perhaps to swing the election to the Republicans.

The 1934 elections assuaged New Dealer fears. The Democrats carried the House of Representatives, in a surprising upsurge, by 322 to 103. But with the NRA faltering, with businessmen rising to the attack and criticism mounting from all quarters, Roosevelt decided in 1935 to shift gears. The First New Deal gave way to the Second New Deal, the Tugwell planners to the Brandeis-Frankfurter reformers.

Professor Felix Frankfurter and Justice Louis Brandeis believed in "compensatory" or "deficit" spending, just like Rexford Tugwell and Raymond Moley, the leader of the so-called Brain Trust. They also endorsed relief and made work—such as the WPA.

The Work Relief Act of April 1935 created a Works Progress Administration, which eventually spent $10.5 billion and created, at its peak, jobs for 3.8 million unemployed. This new work relief —also supervised by Harry Hopkins—paid about twice as much as direct relief. Among its physical achievements were 100,000 bridges and viaducts; repair and building of 110,000 schools, libraries, playgrounds, hospitals, and other structures; innumerable sewerage systems; 500,000 miles of roads and streets. The WPA, too, came in for a lot of criticism. Its workers were called lazy "boondogglers." Pictures were published of men leaning on shovels doing nothing, or huddled around fires.

Despite such criticism, the New Deal reformers, like the New Deal planners, agreed that without the WPA and similar programs the nation would have been in much deeper trouble. Where the two groups within the New Deal differed was on how to make the basic economy more productive. Tugwell would do it through central planning, Brandeis and Frankfurter through regulating business competition and introducing reforms that would narrow the gap between rich and poor.

Bills introduced by the reformers under the Second New Deal were frankly aimed at weakening entrenched greed. The Public Utilities Holding Act, for instance, was expected to reduce the power of monopolies in public utilities such as gas and electricity. In the long run, however, such laws were failures. None stopped the advance of monopolies, which continues to this day.

A bill that had a more positive effect was the National Labor Relations Act, drafted by Senator Robert F. Wagner of New York. The Wagner act, as it was called, was frankly meant to give workers more power in dealing with their bosses. It recognized the right of workers to form unions and bargain with employers. Employers were prohibited from firing anyone for joining a union and from engaging in other unfair labor practices, such as forming their own, company-controlled unions.

The National Labor Relations Board (NLRB), established by the act, enforced these rights. It conducted elections to determine who should represent the workers, if anyone. Whenever a majority of workers in any factory, mine, office, store, voted for a particular union, the employer was obligated to bargain with it. If the employer did something unfair, the NLRB could call him to task and impose penalties on him.

It would be wrong to say that the Wagner act was the reason

unions grew from 4 million to the 20 million members of today. The formation of John L. Lewis' Congress of Industrial Organizations (CIO) in 1935, and the innumerable strikes of 1934–38 gave labor its true momentum. But the Wagner Act did help. By 1945 the NLRB had conducted 24,000 elections among 6 million workers—most of the elections won by the unions. And it had reinstated 300,000 workers who were unjustly fired, with millions of dollars in back pay.

Another goal of the Brandeis-Frankfurter reformers was "soak-the-rich" legislation. Roosevelt had said, "I want to save our system, the capitalistic system." For this "it may be necessary to throw to the wolves the forty-six men who are reported to have incomes in excess of one million dollars a year." To redistribute income in favor of the poor, the reformers proposed higher taxes on big corporations and rich individuals, as well as a stiff inheritance tax that would make it more difficult to inherit large fortunes.

These proposals, however, brought forth so much criticism from business that they had to be modified. Newspaper editors criticized them as a "raw deal" to "soak the successful." What passed, therefore, were levies so modest that they brought in only $250 million additional revenue for the federal government.

The most significant achievement of the "Second Hundred Days" of hectic legislation was a social security bill that put a cushion under poverty. It was more extensive than any known before, and is still on the books. The law provided four types of aid—two through insurance and two paid directly by the government.

Henceforth most employees were to contribute 1 percent of their pay into a compulsory, federally administered pension fund. The employer would match this amount. Out of these monies social security of $10 to $85 a month—depending on previous earnings—would be paid those who retired at age sixty-five. Both the tax and the benefits, of course, have been much increased since then.

Another insurance program was unemployment compensation.

Both the federal government and the states levied taxes on employers to pay for this insurance. When an employee lost his job, he was entitled to a weekly benefit—which varied with each state.

The two other sections of the bill provided direct government payments to those at retirement age who were not eligible for social security; and aid to the blind, the crippled, and dependent mothers and children.

The new social security system clearly was a major step forward. But, like so many other parts of the New Deal, it was a compromise, with obvious defects. "In short," wrote *The New Republic,* "the law is almost a model of what legislation ought not to be."

For one thing, it catered to states' rights and thereby caused inequities as wide as canyons. A blind man might receive $10 a month in one state, $30 a month in another just across the river. An unemployed man or woman might be paid benefits for fifteen weeks in one state, twenty in another.

There were no benefits in case of sickness, no allowances to aid large families, and no medical or health insurance. Too many people were excluded from coverage; among these were farmers, the self-employed, and agricultural laborers. Finally there was the fact that the old-age pensions were not gratuities but compulsory insurance payments over which the recipient exercised no control. By comparison with European standards the bill was generations behind—and still is today, after many amendments.

Nonetheless these reforms drastically changed American life. So did lesser reforms of the Second New Deal. The Walsh-Healey Public Contracts Act prohibited child labor and established a forty-hour week and minimum wages for industries doing business with the government. The Fair Labor Standards Act set maximum hours of work, for industry generally, of forty-four hours a week, tapering down to forty hours two years later. Minimum wages were set at 25 cents an hour, rising to 40 cents after seven years.

The Rural Electrification Administration offered farm communities low-cost loans to string electric power lines to their villages.

It modified rural life in a way that might have pleased the nine-teenth-century Grangers. The Wagner-Steagall housing act, while it resulted in only small amounts of slum clearance and public housing, opened a new dimension in welfare programs.

These and other reforms, whatever their weaknesses in the eyes of social workers and political philosophers, lent a humanistic aura to the New Deal that no Administration in this century has been able to improve on.

Nonetheless the Second New Deal, like the first one, did not abolish poverty—or come close. There were still 10 to 11 million unemployed as of the end of 1938. And despite the WPA and

Farm labor camps. Below: *Sign in Memphis, Tennessee.* Opposite above: *Workers at the Elba camp in Batavia, New York.* Opposite below: *A migrant bean picker at Seabrook Farm, Bridgeton, New Jersey. (Library of Congress)*

compensatory spending, the economy had not yet returned to the production levels of 1929.

On January 4, 1939, the New Deal was gently and officially laid to rest. Roosevelt told Congress, "We have now passed the period of internal conflict in the launching of our program of social reform." The task now, he said, was "to invigorate the processes of recovery in order to preserve our reforms." From here on, the improvements wrought by the Second Hundred Days were to be preserved—not expanded.

By this time the agitation in the streets had already spent itself. The Townsend, Long, and Coughlin movements were dimming memories; farm strikes and eviction struggles occurred only episodically. A revived labor movement, sparked by the CIO sitdown strikes of 1937, was three times as large as in 1933. The search for industrial justice became more orderly and less militant. Roosevelt could back away from his mighty experiment with little fear for his political future.

The summary of New Deal achievements made in mid-1936 by *The New Republic*'s editors applied with equal force in early 1939:

> If one compares it with the measures necessary for a thorough renovation of our society, for creating an economy of abundance, it is sadly deficient, and even, in some respects, reactionary. If one compares it with its own promises and pretensions, and with what it might have done, given the popular support it aroused at the beginning, it is less blameworthy, but still a chapter of lost opportunities.

All the alphabetical agencies, the planning and reforms of the First and Second New Deals, had accomplished something— but far from enough. At the peak of the Great Depression in 1933, 24.9 percent of the labor force were without jobs. In 1938 this had fallen to 19 percent, and in 1939 to 17.2 percent. But one out of six workers out of work was still a staggering figure.

John T. Flynn later wrote of Roosevelt that "the war rescued him." Whatever one may think of Flynn's conservative views, this was an accurate assessment. It was not the FERA, CWA, NRA, PWA, or WPA which finally put America back to work, but the war orders coming from Europe after 1939, and then the war expenditures by the United States itself. The Cold War with the Soviet Union after 1946, which resulted in enormous military spending during the next few decades, stoked the economy and kept Americans at their workbenches thereafter.

17

Minority Poverty

For a quarter of a century after the Second New Deal the problem of poverty receded from the national consciousness. Yesterday's jobless found work. In their modest but improving comfort, Americans forgot the nightmare of the Great Depression —almost as if it had never happened.

The number without work declined to 8 million in 1940, and then finally to a mere 670,000 in 1944. Income on the farm doubled during the war years, as did the gross national product.

The overnight miracle of 1940–45 was due to neither planning nor reform. It was entirely the result of war spending. The government injected vast sums into the economy—$200 billion for munitions, $50 billion for "lend-lease" to foreign allies, more than $20 billion for new factories built from federal revenues but operated by private industry. Roosevelt reported in January 1945 that nearly half of the nation's output was sold to one customer —the federal government.

The government bought 300,000 planes, 65,000 ships, 17 million rifles, 90,000 tanks. The $64 billion spent on munitions in the single year 1944 was many times all the monies spent on New Deal programs from 1933 through 1938. The aim of this un-paralleled spending, of course, was to defeat the Axis. But it was deficit spending and pump priming on an unprecedented scale. Inevitably this had the side effect of shriveling poverty.

The personal income of all workers in 1940 was about $50 billion, in 1945 about $120 billion. One out of seven workers was out of work in 1940, one out of every fifty in 1945. What's more, unlike Europe, not a single inch of United States territory had been bombed, not a single building blown up. The worst wartime hardship back home was the rationing of meats, gasoline, and cigarettes—and people learned how to buy those on the black market.

After World War II quite a few people expected another depression—either like the one in 1921 that followed World War I, or like 1929. It didn't happen. Citizens had $45 billion worth of war bonds tucked away and $100 billion in their savings accounts. That money was there for new washing machines and automobiles.

As important as the consumer spending—in the long run more important—was the enormous amount of military spending. This was something new in American practice. From 1933 to 1937 the highest yearly expenditure for the armed services was less than $1 billion; even as late as 1940 it was less than $1½ billion. But with the Cold War that followed the "hot" one, the figures became astronomical. They ranged from $12 billion in 1948 to $75 billion and $80 billion in recent years. The United States was now allocating ten times as much for military power as for its whole annual budget during the 1930's. The hot war—World War II—cost $400 billion; the Cold War that followed, more than three times as much.

Again, no one planned the Cold War as an antipoverty program. Its stated aim was to "defeat Communism." But spending $1¼ trillion on defense obviously put many, many people to work. Richard P. Oliver of the Bureau of Labor Statistics estimated in 1967 that military spending accounted for 7½ million jobs. And since each employed person makes work for others (through the things he buys), it is obvious that without this spending America would have had another "Great Depression"—as bad as, or worse than, the 1930's.

Children playing in a Harlem backyard. (photograph by Claus Meyer, Black Star)

In any event, a generation of postwar Americans lived in a military-induced prosperity and forgot about the widespread poverty of the 1930's. Economic slumps—five of them since World War II—were now called "recessions," because they were mild compared with those of earlier years. In good times and poor ones, 15 or 20 million union members got a raise every year, and unemployment never was more than an average of 6 percent annually.

Furthermore, the reforms of the New Deal remained to cushion the shocks of unemployment, old age, and adversity—and were even improved upon. The minimum wage went up from 40 cents an hour to 75 cents and, by the end of the 1960's, $1.60. Social security payments increased steadily. So did welfare and unemployment compensation. A "GI Bill of Rights" granted tuition and living allowances for discharged servicemen if they chose to go to college or trade school. Millions did.

Americans forged for themselves the comfortable belief that just about everything that could be done to banish poverty had been done. Perhaps this belief was due to the fact that many people had spread out to the suburbs, where they no longer saw the poor. The poor, said author Michael Harrington, had become "invisible." Or, perhaps it was due to the fact that the nation no longer had "majority poverty," where most people were poor. As economist John Kenneth Galbraith observed, it was now—unlike the 1930's—a "minority poverty."

Visible or invisible, majority or minority, however, there were still tens of millions of poor—their numbers were not negligible. As of 1953, a quarter of the families and other spending units in the country lived on less than $2,000 a year. A study by the Federal Reserve Board in 1954 revealed that more than 14 million families owned no liquid assets to fall back on for a rainy day; that was more than a quarter of the nation. As of 1958, one-fifth of the families averaged less than $1,500 a year, and two-fifths less than $3,500.

The poor of the 1950's and 1960's did not become visible until they began to fight for themselves. Then, all of a sudden, they reemerged in the national consciousness.

On December 1, 1955, a black seamstress, Rosa Parks, took a seat on the Cleveland Avenue bus in Montgomery, Alabama. When the bus driver told her to give the seat to a white man, she refused. Ms. Parks, long active in the National Association for the Advancement of Colored People (NAACP), was arrested—initiating a chain of events no one had anticipated.

Within twenty-four hours the black leaders of Montgomery had proclaimed a boycott of the city buses. Seventeen thousand blacks formed car pools or walked to work—rain or shine—for 381 days rather than accept second-class status any longer.

Among the men who launched the Montgomery Improvement Association, which directed the boycott, was the short, stocky twenty-six-year-old minister of the Dexter Avenue Baptist Church, Martin Luther King, Jr. Until that moment, King's life had been undistinguished. Studious, well-read, a believer in nonviolence, King was the personification of the "new Negro." He had attended the small, integrated Crozer Theological Seminary of Chester, Pennsylvania; had taken his doctorate at Boston University; and returned to his birthplace, Atlanta. From 1947 to 1954 he served in his father's church, until assigned to the one in Montgomery.

As part of the younger generation of blacks, more and more of them college-educated, King thought of religion as something more than an exercise in theology. It was, in his view, also a tool for social change. Before long he had formed a committee to register people for voting and was doing what he could to help the NAACP.

An oratorical spellbinder, King was able to galvanize the Montgomery boycotters to a sense of quiet determination not seen for a long time. When his home was bombed on January 30, 1956, he pleaded with his followers, "Don't go get your weapons. He who lives by the sword will perish by the sword." Shortly thereafter twenty-four ministers, including King, were arrested and convicted of sponsoring the boycott. The young Baptist was sentenced to 140 days in jail and fined $500.

But the boycott continued during the appeal, and in December 1956 the Supreme Court upheld the lower federal courts, which had declared the Alabama law on bus segregation unconstitutional. After more than a year the 17,000 blacks had won their fight—and in the process launched a new movement.

Inspired by King and the events in Montgomery, three militant civil rights forces were soon organizing marches and demonstrations all over the South: King's own Southern Christian Leadership Conference (SCLC), founded in Atlanta by 100 clergymen; the Congress of Racial Equality (CORE), headed by James Farmer, a long-time pacifist; and the Student Nonviolent Coordinating Committee (SNCC), established with King's aid in 1960 and led by such young men as Robert Parris Moses, John Lewis, and James Foreman.

Risking their lives frequently and going to jail even more frequently (King himself was arrested more than a dozen times), these "true believers" led hundreds of freedom marches, bus rides, and sit-ins in the next seven years. They demanded equality for the black man and enforcement of the Supreme Court decision on school desegregation. Thousands of them fell to policemen's clubs or were arrested—300 in Selma, Alabama, alone from September 15 to October 2, 1963.

Black and white sympathizers were murdered. Churches were bombed. Police dogs were called out against demonstrators in

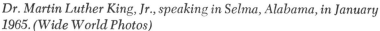

Dr. Martin Luther King, Jr., speaking in Selma, Alabama, in January 1965. (Wide World Photos)

Birmingham. Innumerable reprisals were visited upon black militants by "White Citizens Councils." But the agitation continued, climaxing in the 1963 "March on Washington for Freedom and Jobs," which drew 200,000 people, and the walk from Selma to Montgomery two years later.

The black revolt concentrated at first on the issue of social and political equality—equal treatment on buses and in restaurants and hotels, desegregation of schools, the right to vote. But after many of these rights were partially won, the focus shifted to equality in jobs and income. As King put it, it didn't do the black man much good to have the right to sit at a lunch counter if he didn't have the price of a hamburger in his pocket.

There was something reminiscent about the poverty of black people in the 1950's. It resembled in many respects that of the foreign-born a few decades back. The foreign-born had been immigrants from outside the country; the blacks of the 1950's and 1960's were "internal immigrants"—large numbers were moving from the South to the North, and from villages and rural areas to the cities. They were shifting from farming and sharecropping to factory labor.

In 1910 three-quarters of the 10 million Afro-Americans lived on farms, and all but 800,000 in the South. But with so many jobs open in the factories during and after the two world wars, there was a steady migration to the cities, and to industry. By 1968, 69 percent of the 21.5 million blacks lived in metropolitan areas, almost half outside the South. In some northern cities blacks had become a majority of the population—in Newark and Washington, D.C., for instance. Along with the black migration, incidentally, was an influx of the Spanish-speaking, especially from Puerto Rico. There were 100,000 Puerto Ricans in New York City in 1940, and 700,000 twenty years later.

The blacks lived in the same kind of slums as the immigrants of yesteryear, slums such as Harlem in New York, the South Side in Chicago, Watts in Los Angeles. They were the last to be hired for a job, the first to be fired. Their income was much lower than that of whites—only slightly more than half—and their rate of unemployment usually two to three times as high.

A highly publicized federal commission that investigated riots in the black ghettos during the 1960's found that there was a "culture of poverty" caused by "unemployment and family disorganization. . . ." That culture inevitably included the usual vices of poverty—prostitution, dope addiction, casual sexual affairs, violent crime—and created "an environmental jungle characterized by personal insecurity and tension."

Few people were concerned about this "culture of poverty" in the black sections of the major cities until it erupted into mass violence. The focus of attention until then was on civil rights and the various activities in Southern cities such as Montgomery, Birmingham, Selma. Suddenly, however, the focus changed to black poverty in the cities of the North.

Minor incidents of real or alleged police brutality in 1964 spurred violent outbreaks in New York, Rochester, Philadelphia, Jersey City, Elizabeth, Paterson. The following year disorders broke out in the Watts section of Los Angeles during which 4,000 persons were arrested, 34 killed, hundreds injured, and $35 million in property destroyed. In 1966, when police in Chicago refused to turn on fire hydrants for black children during a hot July day, there were riots in that city which necessitated the calling out of 4,200 national guardsmen. The summer after, there were riots in Newark, Detroit, and almost 150 other cities in which tens of millions of dollars' worth of property was burned down and thousands of blacks arrested. A survey of seventy-five of these disturbances showed 83 killed and 1,897 injured.

The black rebellion reached another climax less than a year later, in April 1968, after the tragic assassination of Martin Luther King, Jr. King was in Memphis planning a demonstration on behalf of black garbagemen who were striking for union recognition and higher wages. He was cut down by a rifle shot. Within a few hours the outrage of black people—and others—reached mammoth proportions. Mostly it took the form of silent disbelief as the nation mourned its martyr.

A man is taken into custody during riot in Detroit in the summer of 1967. (Wide World Photos)

But in many places the outrage spilled over to violence. In Washington, D.C., within sight of the White House, scores of buildings were put to the torch. There were riots in Chicago and many other cities. The toll in dead was less than in the summer of 1967, but the government was forced to call out more than 26,500 soldiers and 47,000 national guardsmen. "Not since the Civil War," commented *The New York Times,* "has this country experienced an epidemic of domestic violence as widespread as it was this weekend."

The killing, looting, vandalism, and arson, especially in 1967 and 1968, disturbed many Americans. A vocal few blamed Stokely Carmichael and his cry for black power. When Carmichael, leader of SNCC, had first used the words "black power," they had a hypnotic effect; they gave black people a feeling of pride and hope. Yet, it would be wrong to say they had anything to do with causing the violence of those years. To sober people it was obvious that the black rebellion had been spontaneous—leaderless.

That so many people in so many places should have risen in anger proved that there was a widespread desperation.

The agitation in the streets was accompanied, inevitably, by a growth of public concern. Writers began to publish an increasing number of books and articles on the prevailing poverty, particularly of blacks, but also of other Americans. Political leaders began to cock an ear to what was going on.

In the 1950's and 1960's, just as in the early part of the century, there were some men of conscience who demanded that something be done. Two writers who had considerable influence on the dialogue over poverty were John Kenneth Galbraith and, especially, Michael Harrington.

Galbraith, an economics professor, published a book in 1958 with the deceptive title *The Affluent Society.* There was now a new type of poverty, he said, amidst national affluence. There were islands of privation in the ghettos, and in the worked-out mining areas of West Virginia, even while the nation as a whole was unbelievably prosperous. But for those who were poor it was just as painful a society as any in the past.

Galbraith's book, written in witty, nonacademic language, opened the door to a new awareness of the subject. As yet, however, it didn't penetrate deeply enough, though it did inspire many other new books under such titles as *Poverty Amid Affluence,* and *Poverty in the Affluent Society.*

Michael Harrington's book *The Other America,* published in 1962, had a greater impact. Harrington, a young socialist, showed there was another America invisible to most people—the America of the poor. In a lively writing style, he made the poor seem real. He described life in a jail, where he himself had been put after a civil rights demonstration. He wrote about the "rejects" who lost their jobs through automation and plant shutdowns; and about welfare recipients, the sick, the alcoholic, and, above all, the blacks—"If You're Black, Stay Back." The poor, he said, "tend to become increasingly invisible," but they exist and in large numbers.

Poverty, Harrington argued, was not merely a lack of money.

Two residents of a New York City men's shelter on the Bowery. (photograph by Carole Bertol)

It was a way of life, a subculture of people who had little opportunity to climb out of their lowly status. *The Other America* drove home the idea that nothing society was then doing—public housing, welfare, or copious federal spending—really percolated down to the invisible poor.

Harrington's book had a considerable effect on men of power. It was published a year after John F. Kennedy became President. At the time, there were many "freedom rides" being conducted in the South, and a surge of student activity against social injustice and war. Kennedy's inaugural address responded to these pressures: "If a free society," he said, "cannot help the many who are poor, it cannot save the few who are rich."

Kennedy was preparing an antipoverty program to present to Congress when he was assassinated in Dallas in November 1963. Vice-President Lyndon Johnson took over the responsibility.

18

The Unwon War

Lyndon Baines Johnson, a tall Texan, was the first southern President in a century. He had come to Washington in 1931, at the age of twenty-three, as secretary to a conservative Texas congressman. Later, however, he became a New Dealer and served as a state director of the National Youth Administration under its liberal chief, Aubrey Williams. Subsequently he ran in the Tenth Congressional District of Texas as a New Deal candidate. His six opponents all hated Franklin Roosevelt—and Johnson beat them all. Roosevelt liked "LBJ" and treated him, it is said, like an adopted son.

After FDR's death Johnson shifted to the conservative side. He became chummy with the construction and oil interests in his home state, and was noted for caution and compromise. In August 1948 he won a primary fight for nomination to the United States Senate, by a mere eighty-seven votes. There was some scandal connected with this event—202 ballots mysteriously appeared from a remote precinct. Nonetheless LBJ was in the Senate, and two years later became whip of his Democratic Party. Two years after that, he graduated to become the Democratic floor leader.

In the Senate, Johnson voted consistently against civil rights legislation—until 1957. He had the image for many people of the

187

wheeler-dealer, who worked closely with Republican President Eisenhower and southern conservatives such as Senator Richard Russell. He seemed like a man with no commitment except to his personal career.

He did vote for some liberal measures such as higher minimum wages and social security, but when it came to questions of oil or natural gas he was always with big business. When Kennedy chose him as his running mate in 1960, organized labor was so horrified that some of its leaders—Walter Reuther, for instance—considered bolting the Democratic Party.

Yet, Johnson was in the Executive Office only five days when he proposed "a civil rights law so that we can move forward to eliminate from this nation every trace of discrimination and oppression that is based upon race or color." Forty-two days later, in a forty-minute "State of the Union" message, he made the most ringing appeal on poverty heard in a quarter of a century:

> Unfortunately, many Americans live on the outskirts of hope, some because of their poverty and some because of their color, and all too many because of both. Our task is to help

A Kentucky hollow, home of one-time farmers turned miners who are now unemployed. (Black Star)

replace their despair with opportunity. And this Administration today, here and now, declares unconditional war on poverty in America. . . . It will not be a short or easy struggle, no single weapon or strategy will suffice, but we shall not rest until that war is won.

Within a few months Johnson was talking of the "Great Society" which would bring "an end to poverty and racial injustice . . . in our time." It was inspiring talk—all the more so because it was assumed that Johnson would be able to guide new bills through Congress more easily than Kennedy might have.

Johnson's Great Society proposals ranged all over the lot; they included a hefty $11 billion tax cut; aid for schools, libraries, and nursing homes; a mass transit bill; higher unemployment compensation and minimum wages. But four laws in particular affected the needy: medical care for the aged, a new type of education bill, a voting rights act, and an omnibus antipoverty law.

The "Medicare" bill of 1965 provided older people with 90 days of hospitalization plus 100 days of nursing home care afterward. The aged person paid only $40 of the initial hospital costs and $10 each day after the sixtieth day. For $3 a month he could also cover himself for the costs of doctors' care, X-rays, and similar expenditures.

The aid-to-education law allotted $1 billion for aid to school districts that had a large number of children from poor families. The Higher Education Act made available a couple of billion dollars for loans to college students, as well as for adult education and grants to libraries.

The Voting Rights Bill of 1965 was not included in Johnson's original plan. But after the uproar over the civil rights march in Selma, where a Unitarian minister, James Reeb, was killed, Johnson decided to press for voting changes too. For a long time black people had been deprived of the vote by being forced to take literacy tests and pay poll taxes. Somehow they seldom passed the literacy tests, given by white examiners; and the poll taxes usually made it too expensive to vote. Both these devices were now abolished, and Congress authorized federal examiners to register black voters in places where there was a pattern of discrimination.

The core of the Great Society, however, was the Economic Opportunity Act of August 1964, commonly called the "anti-poverty law." Vice-President Hubert Humphrey called it the "quiet revolution." He and others claimed that it would banish poverty forever. The richest country in the world was finally mounting "the only war worth fighting."

But the law itself was not as far-reaching as it sounded. It offered no additional aid, for instance, to the 8 million helpless poor—those on general assistance, the blind, dependent children, the aged who were not insured under social security. Instead it concentrated on young people and certain social services.

Title I of the antipoverty law created a "job corps" for 100,000 youth between sixteen and twenty-one. Like the CCC of the New Deal, these young people were paid to do conservation work and improve their education. Another 200,000 youth were given "work-training," to prepare them for jobs. A "work-study" program offered fifteen hours of work per week to 140,000 college students of low-income families. The aim of all this was to help the school dropout, as well as college students whose families were too poor to support them.

The second major feature of the bill was community action. In a sense this was like Jane Addams' work of seven decades earlier, except that it was the federal government, rather than the social worker, doing it. "Operation Head Start" gave pre-school training to 750,000 disadvantaged children. Lawyers were hired to furnish legal services for the poor. Hundreds of neighborhood centers were established. Some money was allotted to help the forgotten Indians and migrant workers.

There was more to this omnibus bill. Loans were given to farmers, cooperatives, and small businessmen (about $150 million). Adult education classes were started for those who had not completed school. And young volunteers were enrolled in "Volunteers in Service to America"—VISTA. The task of VISTA was to put these volunteers to work on a variety of jobs in poor areas, such as cleanup, painting, and the like.

Johnson's war on poverty was breathtaking in the diversity of its projects and the millions of people affected. But, as Dr. King argued, it was not a "war" but a "skirmish." All told, only $800 million was appropriated for it in the first year—less than 2 per-cent of what was then being spent for defense. The amount was doubled the next year, but it was still not very large. Even if one includes the four-year authorization of $7 billion for public housing, the "model cities" projects, the public works programs for the eleven-state Appalachia area—even if all this is included

A teacher in Project Head Start directs a music lesson in a New York City public school. (Wide World Photos)

VISTA members help carry out a voter registration drive in a Laredo, Texas, barrio (neighborhood) where many of the poor live. (Wide World Photos)

—the antipoverty program of Lyndon Johnson's administration was a whisper of what was needed.

Critics made this point repeatedly. "The present poverty program," wrote Christopher Jencks in *The New Republic*, "is mainly an extension and amplification of policies established under previous Administrations." Its most "conspicuous fact," he continued, was "the elimination not of poverty but of ignorance, incompetence and so forth. The problem may have been redefined, but the solutions have not."

Three years after the war on poverty had started, *Business Week* noted that "both the number of people on welfare and the cost of supporting them are rising, despite prosperity, a Great Society, and a war on poverty. In 1956, about 5.8 million Americans lived on 'the welfare' at a cost of $3 billion. . . . In 1966, there were eight million on the rolls and the bill was $6.5 billion." By January 1968, there were 8.6 million needy

Americans on relief—one of every twenty-three citizens—and by the end of 1970, more than 13 million.

In Cook County, Illinois—mostly Chicago—6 percent of the population existed on welfare, 82 percent of them blacks. The average grant per person in Illinois was $41.85 a month for food, rent, clothing, and all other expenses, except medical aid. By the federal government's own measurement of poverty, this was only a third of what a single person needed, and two-thirds of what a family of four required. In Mississippi the average monthly dole was $9.35, in Alabama $12.75.

Senator Joseph S. Clark of Pennsylvania, who toured impoverished homes in Washington, D.C., and the Mississippi Delta in 1967, recorded stark instances of "starvation in the affluent society." Five blocks from the Capitol, on Defrees Street, he talked with a seven-year-old boy who had soup for breakfast and soup for lunch, nothing more. A community action worker who guided Clark and Senator Robert Kennedy around the area commented: "There are hundreds of others in this neighborhood who get up in the morning hungry and who go to bed at night hungry. It's been that way ever since I've been here, years and years."

Farther south, in the heart of the Delta, "we found a mother of fifteen children," Clark wrote, "nursing a three-day-old child which she had delivered herself. There was no food in the house, she said, and no money. She didn't know what she would do." Near Greenville, Mississippi, he came across a "tumbledown collection of shacks ironically called Freedom City, housing the families of displaced plantation workers. . . . In this appalling squalor were forty-eight children who subsisted entirely on grits, rice, soybeans, and 'whatever is donated,' plus the customary one can of meat per month. Eggs, milk, and fruit juice, the mothers told me, were unknown."

A group of distinguished doctors who made a similar trip to the Delta told a Senate subcommittee that they "saw children whose nutritional and medical condition we can only describe as shocking. . . . In child after child we saw evidence of vitamin and mineral deficiencies; serious untreated skin infections and ulcerations; eye and ear diseases; the prevalence of bacterial and parasitic disease. . . . We saw homes with children who are lucky to eat one meal a day. . . ."

Dr. Donald E. Gatch told an antipoverty hearing in November 1967 that underfed black youngsters in South Carolina were dying of hookworm, roundworm, and other parasitic diseases. A study of 212 persons in Beaufort County revealed that two-thirds were suffering from parasites, including 90 percent of the children under five. "There's just no damn sense in this country to have a bunch of hungry people. But the hunger and parasite problem isn't on anybody's priority lists."

A still more damning indictment was made by a committee of twenty-five prominent people who made a study of hunger for Walter Reuther's Citizens Crusade Against Poverty. The committee charged that there were between 10 and 14½ million people living in actual hunger and malnutrition—and "the situation is worsening." "If you will look," said the report, "you find America is a shocking place. No other western country permits such a large proportion of its people to endure the lives we press on our poor. To make four-fifths of a nation more affluent than any people in history, we have degraded one-fifth mercilessly."

There were plenty of ideas on how to solve the problem of poverty. A number of economists urged the government to pass laws for a "guaranteed annual income." The government itself would pay a citizen the difference between his earnings and the "guaranteed" minimum. Some proposed that the guaranteed annual income should be between $3,500 and $4,000 for a family of four. That would cost the government somewhere between $11 billion and $25 billion a year. Others suggested a figure of $5,500 (and later $6,500).

Professor Milton Friedman of the University of Chicago proposed a "negative income tax." Those earning less than the poverty level would pay no taxes *to* the government but would receive payments *from* it.

Johnson, however, accepted none of these ideas.

Coincident with the war on poverty, the nation became involved in a "shooting war." The undeclared war in Vietnam was to be the second costliest war in American history. Month by

month, President Johnson's attention became further riveted on
this war, and both he and his colleagues lost interest in the
antipoverty war.

Before long the President and Congress were talking of aus-
terity, and cutbacks in social programs. The country was spending
$25 billion to $30 billion a year on the war in Vietnam; its leaders
didn't think there was money left for a war on poverty at the
same time.

The Great Society lapsed into a coma two years after its birth.

Lyndon B. Johnson decided not to run for President in 1968.
In the stormy election that followed, Republican Richard M.
Nixon defeated Democrat Hubert Humphrey by a scant 500,000
votes. Nixon, a Quaker by birth, was generally believed to be
an archconservative. Certainly he had never distinguished himself as a reformer, and he had little following in either organized
labor or the black communities.

It was Nixon, however, who proposed the most sweeping
change in the structure of welfare since the New Deal. His program, drafted by a liberal professor, Patrick Moynihan, divided
the poor into three categories. For the first, adults in need—the
aged, blind, and disabled—it proposed no change, except a small
increase in benefits. The big changes were for the other two—
families with dependent children, and the working poor.

Citizens covered by Aid to Families with Dependent Children
(AFDC) comprised almost three-quarters of those receiving assistance. According to Nixon, the average benefit for a family of
four on welfare was $171 a month. But it varied greatly: in New
Jersey such a family might receive $263 a month, in Mississippi
$39. What the President proposed was to abolish this ancient
system, which left the ultimate decisions in the hands of the
states and local communities. Instead the federal government
would place a floor under welfare, so that every family of four
would be guaranteed a minimum of $1,600 a year plus food
stamps. Those getting more would continue getting more; those
getting less would be brought up to that minimum—$133.33 a
month.

In addition to the floor under welfare, there were a number of other important changes. One was the junking of the means test. People applying for relief had had to submit, under the old system, to a humiliating investigation—they had to prove they had no means of support. Under the Nixon Family Assistance Program (FAP) an applicant would simply file a statement of need. He would not have to prove his need, any more than if he applied for social security or unemployment compensation.

Another significant change was that the plan would be administered centrally from Washington. It would be handled by a "Family Assistance Agency" of the Department of Health, Education, and Welfare.

Still another innovation of the Nixon-Moynihan scheme was the provision for aid to the working poor—those who had jobs but earned poverty wages. The 2 million families in this category would also receive $1,600, less a portion of what they earned in wages, up to a combined maximum of $3,920 a year.

The President called his antipoverty package "workfare"— creating a bridge "from welfare to work." It was not a guaranteed annual income, he said, because it would not be paid to an able-bodied person who refused a job.

In presenting FAP to Congress, Nixon called it a matter of top priority. But 1969 passed, 1970 passed, 1971 passed—and nothing happened. The program was redrafted somewhat, to guarantee $2,200 a year, then $2,400 a year (but no food stamps). Still there was no action.

One of the reasons for the inaction was that FAP satisfied neither the conservatives nor the liberals. Conservatives liked the workfare part of it, but they were unhappy with the fact that control would be taken out of the hands of the local governments.

Liberals liked the minimum-standards aspects of FAP and the abolition of the means test. But they were greatly disturbed by the fact that for the vast majority of welfare clients there would be no increase in benefits.

The group that protested most strongly was the 125,000-member National Welfare Rights Organization (NWRO). This was a militant organization formed in 1967 by Dr. George Wiley, a black chemistry professor at Syracuse University. The NWRO didn't like workfare, and wanted a guaranteed annual income of $6,500 a year instead of $2,200 or $2,400.

Perhaps the major reason why there was no sense of urgency about FAP was that Congress was thinking of other matters— the recession that began in 1969–70, the 6-percent unemployment, the 5- and 6-percent rise in prices each year, and the war in Vietnam.

Late in 1972 Congress killed FAP. The Democrats blamed it on the Republican President; Nixon blamed it on the Democrats. It was a dead issue either way. Very likely, FAP, or something like it, will be revived in the next few years; and if so it will be an improvement over the present welfare system. Its benefits, however, will still be too meager to abolish poverty, and it would do painfully little about the culture that surrounds poverty.

The defeat of FAP punctuates the fact that the richest nation in the world has been unable—or unwilling—to erase want and privation, even though many good people have tried to lead such a crusade. Since William Penn's Holy Experiment there have been any number of reformers and radicals with all kinds of plans as to how poverty could be abolished. Yet the plague is still with us.

Too many Americans have found it easier to hide behind arguments that the poor are unfit for a better fate, than to mount a real campaign against inequality and destitution. They have been ready to believe that the poor are "cheaters" or "lazy," or that they have illegitimate children only to get more welfare money. But these arguments are untrue to begin with, and serve merely as excuses to escape responsibility. The nation is preaching brotherhood but is not really practicing it.

Yet, on the other side, it is evident that every time the poor have fought for themselves they have made some progress. Their heroic effort during the American Revolution brought significant gains. Their labor parties in the 1820's sparked many reforms which made the lot of the lowly more bearable. The trade unions,

This family in Virginia receives emergency food and medical services from the federal government. (photograph by Stuart Oring, Office of Economic Opportunity)

first organized in the 1790's, have won higher wages and innumerable other benefits throughout American history. The granges, the alliances, the People's Party, toward the end of the nineteenth century were responsible eventually for a host of improvements. Organizations of unemployed, farmer groups, reform and radical movements of a dozen types, also made their contributions toward containing or reducing poverty.

Because of all of their efforts, the plight of the underprivileged, bad as it is, is not as bad as it was a generation ago or five generations ago—or as bad as it is in other countries. An impoverished man or woman in the United States today usually owns a television set, a refrigerator, sometimes an auto, and other amenities the poor of yesterday did not enjoy. He or she is certainly at a higher living standard than the poor of countries like India or Brazil. Moreover, the percentage of people in poverty in the United States is smaller than in the 1930's or in 1893 or 1837, when there were major depressions. In absolute terms, although far, far too many are still hungry, the conditions of the poor are better than they used to be.

Poverty, however, is something relative; a person is judged to be poor by comparison with other people, as well as by his inability to satisfy elementary needs. In that relative sense the situation is bleak. The gap between those in want and those at the top of the ladder is still as great as—or greater than—it was generations ago.

The impoverished live in a climate of hopelessness. They do not see themselves rising to a higher status. They lack the opportunity for an adequate education. They are unable to find jobs, in part because the educational requirements are now higher. They are poorly housed, poorly fed—millions are still only a step removed from actual starvation. Worse still, there are large numbers of families who have lived in poverty for generations and do not imagine any prospect of climbing out of that poverty in the foreseeable future.

This is America's unwon war—the war against poverty. If it is to be won in the years to come, it will only be because the poor themselves, and people of conscience who sympathize with them, will make a much more sustained effort to abolish poverty than anything known in the past.

Books for Further Reading

ABBOTT, EDITH. *Historical Aspects of the Immigration Problem.* Chicago, University of Chicago Press, 1926.

———. *Public Assistance.* Vols. 1–5. New York, Russell & Russell Publishers, 1966.

ADAMS, GRACE. *Workers on Relief.* New Haven, Yale University Press, 1939.

BAGDIKIAN, BEN H. *In the Midst of Plenty: A New Report on the Poor in America.* Boston, Beacon Press, 1964.

BENNETT, LERONE, JR. *What Manner of Man: A Memorial Biography of Martin Luther King, Jr.* Chicago, Johnson Publishing, 1968.

BREMER, ROBERT H. *American Philanthropy.* Chicago, University of Chicago Press, 1960.

———. *From the Depths.* New York, New York University Press, 1956.

BUCK, SOLON J. *The Agrarian Crusade.* New Haven, Yale University Press, 1920.

CREECH, MARGARET. *Three Centuries of Poor Law Administration: A Study of Legislation in Rhode Island.* Chicago, University of Chicago Press, 1936.

DU BOIS, W. E. B. *Black Reconstruction.* New York, Harcourt, Brace, 1935.

FERMAN, LOUIS A., et. al., eds. *Poverty in America: A Book of Readings*, rev. ed. Ann Arbor, University of Michigan Press, 1968.

GALBRAITH, JOHN KENNETH. *The Affluent Society*. Boston, Houghton Mifflin Company, 1958.

HARRINGTON, MICHAEL. *The Other America*. New York, The Macmillan Company, 1962.

HILL, HERBERT, AND GREENBERG, JACK. *Citizen's Guide to Desegregation*. Boston, Beacon Press, 1955.

HOFSTADTER, RICHARD. *The Age of Reform: From Bryan to FDR*. New York, Alfred A. Knopf, 1955.

HUMPHREY, HUBERT H. *War on Poverty*. New York, McGraw-Hill, 1964.

HUNTER, ROBERT. *Poverty*. New York, The Macmillan Company, 1907.

JAMESON, J. FRANKLIN. *The American Revolution Considered as a Social Event*. Princeton, Princeton University Press, 1926.

JONES, MALDWYN ALLEN. *American Immigration*. Chicago, University of Chicago Press, 1960.

JORNS, AUGUSTE. *The Quakers as Pioneers in Social Work*. New York, The Macmillan Company, 1931.

KING, MARTIN LUTHER, JR. *Stride Toward Freedom*. New York, Harper & Brothers, 1958.

LARNER, JEREMY, AND HOWE, IRVING, eds. *Poverty: Views from the Left*. New York, William Morrow, 1971.

LENS, SIDNEY. *Poverty: America's Enduring Paradox*. New York, Thomas Y. Crowell Company, 1969.

MITCHELL, BROADUS. *Depression Decade*. New York, Rinehart, 1947.

MOHL, RAYMOND A. *Poverty in New York: 1783–1825*. New York, Oxford University Press, 1971.

MORRIS, RICHARD B. *Government and Labor in Early America*. New York, Columbia University Press, 1946.

MOYNIHAN, DANIEL P., ed. *On Understanding Poverty: Perspectives from the Social Sciences*. New York, Basic Books, 1969.

PHILLIPS, ULRICH B. *American Negro Slavery*. New York, Appleton-Century-Crofts, 1918.

QUARLES, BENJAMIN. *The Negro in the Making of America*. New York, The Macmillan Company, 1964.

Report of the National Advisory Commission on Civil Disorders. New York, Bantam Books, 1968.

RIIS, JACOB. *How the Other Half Lives.* New York, Dover Publications, 1971.

ROCHESTER, ANNA. *The Populist Movement in the United States.* New York, International Publishers, 1943.

SELIGMAN, BEN B. *Poverty as a Public Issue.* New York, The Free Press, 1968.

SEXTON, PATRICIA C. *Spanish Harlem.* New York, Harper and Row, 1965.

SHANNON, DAVID A. *The Great Depression.* Englewood Cliffs, N.J., Prentice-Hall, 1960.

SIMON, ARTHUR. *Faces of Poverty.* New York, The Macmillan Company, 1968.

STAMPP, KENNETH M. *The Peculiar Institution.* New York, Alfred A. Knopf. 1956.

TYLER, ALICE FELT. *Freedom's Ferment.* Minneapolis, University of Minnesota Press, 1944.

WECTER, DIXON. *The Age of the Great Depression.* New York, The Macmillan Company, 1941.

WEISBROD, BURTON. *The Economics of Poverty: An American Paradox.* Englewood Cliffs, N.J., Prentice-Hall, 1965.

Index

(Page numbers in italics refer to illustrations.)

About the Author

Sidney Lens, a former editor of *Liberation* magazine, is the author of a dozen books on foreign affairs and on American labor. He received the Midland Author's Award in 1970 for his adult book on poverty, *Poverty: America's Enduring Paradox.* His articles have appeared in numerous periodicals, including *Harper's, The Progressive, The Nation, Rotarian, Harvard Business Review,* and *Commonweal.*

Mr. Lens has been a union official most of his life, and is one of the founders of the national peace movement. An avid traveler, he has visited ninety-four countries. He and his wife make their home in Northbrook, Illinois.

301.44   Lens, Sidney
Len
p   Poverty: yesterday
          and today